Julia McGuinness is a writ author of *Creative Praying in* *Most of Midlife* (SPCK, 2006), as well as writing for Redemptorist's 'Sunday Links' and the *Church Times*. She has a private counselling practice, and as a Myers-Briggs practitioner also runs workshops in secular environments and church settings. She is a Reader at St Thomas and All Saints' Ellesmere Port with St Lawrence's Stoak Village, a parish with a wide range of churchmanship across its different services.

GROWING SPIRITUALLY WITH THE MYERS-BRIGGS® MODEL

Julia McGuinness

First published in Great Britain in 2009

Society for Promoting Christian Knowledge
36 Causton Street
London SW1P 4ST

British Library Cataloguing-in-Publication Data
A catalogue record for this book is available from the British Library

ISBN 978–0–281–05982–9

1 3 5 7 9 10 8 6 4 2

Typeset by Graphicraft Limited, Hong Kong
Printed in Great Britain by Ashford Colour Press

Contents

1

Introducing spiritual direction and the Myers-Briggs® model

---◆◆◆---

The self-guided soul is always prey to delusion.
(Gilbert Shaw)

God leads each one a different way.
(St Teresa of Avila)

Let us run with perseverance the race marked out for us.
(Hebrews 12.1b)

Destinations and directions

The lorry was stuck. Wedged between a wall and a hedge on the narrow village lane, its driver could neither proceed on his journey nor turn back the way he had come. It took several hours and police assistance to manoeuvre the vehicle free.

The age of satellite navigation has heralded chaos on some British roads, as drivers of heavy goods vehicles turn into tiny country lanes in dutiful obedience to 'satnav' instructions, and soon find they can go no further. In summer 2007, the Vale of Glamorgan Council introduced a new road sign at the turn-off to one Welsh village, warning lorry drivers to ignore any satnav directions to drive down it.

Following an unsuitable route can be time-consuming and costly, and not only for the driver concerned. Blocked roads and damage to residents' garden walls or hedges bring frustration all round. It's not enough simply to set a destination. The directions need to be appropriate for the one travelling.

In recent years, the concept of the spiritual journey has gained momentum amid growing disenchantment with the promise of materialism and scientific progress to satisfy our deeper hunger for meaning and purpose in our lives. For some, the spiritual journey is an individual venture with no focused objective. They set out on a quest into the unknown, ready to explore different avenues and follow wherever desire, need or curiosity lead. Those on the Christian journey look with faith beyond earthly pathways towards a heavenly destination. They are on a pilgrimage into the presence of their Maker. But what is true of road travel also applies to spiritual journeying: knowing where we're going is not the same as identifying the best route to get us there.

A journey of growth

Christians share a glorious destiny. As St Augustine of Hippo put it, 'We have been made to know God and enjoy him for ever.' Responding to God's invitation through Christ into his Kingdom means a journey into holiness in preparation for our heavenly home. We are to be 'transformed into Christ's likeness with ever-increasing glory', as Paul tells the Corinthian Christians.[1]

Fundamentally, this is a process of reconnection. We are first and foremost reconnected to God, as the destructive consequences of rebellious self-centred living are reconciled by Jesus' sacrifice on the Cross, and our spiritual deadness is enlivened by the release of his indwelling Spirit. We are also no longer out of sorts with ourselves. Once divided within, we pushed away aspects of ourselves we could not bear to look at. Now we can be at peace, knowing we are completely accepted and forgiven. What was denied or distorted can be healed and integrated under the loving light of Christ.

Reconnecting to God's heart leads us to desire a deeper connection with others, as we learn to love and value our fellow human beings, and have a renewed care for their welfare. Finally, we reconnect with our wider world. Where we may have been insensitive or indifferent to our environment, we now recognize it as God's Creation, to be cherished through our responsible stewardship.

Becoming whole thus comprises a four-fold movement into renewed relationships with God, ourselves, others and our environment.

Help on the Way

Since the Christian journey is one of reconnection, it is clearly not a solo trip for spiritual lone rangers. Anne Long describes discipleship as directed living.[2] So who or what does the directing?

Primarily our director is the Holy Spirit, whose inner work in prompting, enlightening, guiding, convicting and comforting is the birthright of every Christian. But in order to stay on the Way, we need the twin tracks of inner prompting and outer guidance running alongside and in harmony with one another.

The two key sources of guidance are God's written word, the Bible, and the wisdom of other Christians, through formal teaching and lived example. This has been so since Jesus himself gathered a group of disciples around him, and taught them by both opening up the Scriptures and demonstrating his own personal holiness.

Paul mentored Timothy, and wrote letters to church communities to address the practical issues these fledgling fellowships were facing. They needed mature insight to discern the Way of Christ through particular dilemmas and choices on the road to wholeness.

The Church's monastic period during the third and fourth centuries led to the emergence of a more formal tradition of spiritual direction, as Christians withdrew from the bustle and corruption of city life to devote themselves to discipleship in the Egyptian and Syrian deserts. To offset the potential excesses and imbalances of individualism and acknowledge the Christian call for connectedness to community, there developed the practice of finding a spiritual director or 'abba' for one-to-one guidance in staying on track.

Down the ages, the emerging tradition of spiritual direction became more generally associated with the Church's Catholic wing, incorporating the formal hearing of confession as one element in its practice. Within the last thirty years or so, however, the landscape has been changing again: spiritual direction has come into fashion.

Spiritual direction in the twenty-first century

Perhaps the new impetus is not so surprising: confidence in the direction offered by religious institutions seems to be lessening almost as fast as the desire for spiritual guidance and experience increases. The growth of 'Mind Body Spirit' fairs and the plethora of related self-help literature in our bookshops give some indication of the spiritual appetites underlying our secular society.

Spanning the interface between Church and market-place is the burgeoning retreat movement. The growing popularity of retreats may be symptomatic of a widespread need for respite from the stresses of fast-paced modern living. But in an age that enshrines the right to exercise individual choice, there is clearly an appeal for those within the Church seeking opportunities to pursue a more personal pilgrimage – or perhaps simply to escape from the relentlessness of an over-busy church programme.

The recovery of a sense of the individual is in many ways a positive. It redresses the balance against the bias of large religious groupings towards a one-size-fits-all model for spiritual growth. Sometimes we can conform to the norm as a way of pushing away the personal spiritual challenges. At other times we may find ourselves unsettled, resentful or even fearful of being cast in a particular church mould, aware it is unhelpful for us personally, but unsure of where that leaves us.

Jesus' own choice of disciples affirms the inclusion of diverse personalities in God's Kingdom: reading the story of their lives and letters in the New Testament, it's clear the maturing John looked very different from the maturing Peter. And Paul's letters urge believers to imitate his example of commitment, not impersonate his style of expression. The resurgence of interest in spiritual direction today is also characterized by a more inclusive approach regarding those involved as directors. Laity as well as clergy are being encouraged to offer spiritual direction, especially as its practice develops away from the *de facto* inclusion of formal confession.

Gordon Jeff, who founded SPIDIR (the Spiritual Direction Network) in the UK in the late 1970s, envisages a whole 'reservoir of listening, spiritually receptive people, lay or ordained, women or men, whose sensitivity can be developed'.[3] SPIDIR has worked on providing this through initiating training and appropriate support.

Our own generation has seen some movement towards redefining the term 'spiritual director' itself, as a gesture towards freeing it from earlier authoritarian connotations. Kenneth Leech has used 'soul-friend' to underline the director's status as fellow-traveller, not elevated guru.[4] The term is also integral to the Celtic Christian tradition, which has gained wider recognition in recent years, perhaps through the appeal of its more community-friendly, non-hierarchical structure.

Margaret Guenther presents the spiritual director as a midwife, alongside and facilitating the believer as she or he struggles to bring to birth new spiritual life ready to emerge from within. She also highlights spiritual direction as simple hospitality, the offer of a safe space to explore new avenues in a climate of openness and acceptance.[5]

For Gordon Jeff, the emphasis is on a low-key, one-to-one encounter, three or four times a year. The spiritual director listens prayerfully as the Christian talks through his or her spiritual journey. This then leads to mutual discernment of key issues and areas needing specific attention.

Demystifying the process in this way makes spiritual direction more accessible, and maintains the focus on the individual's active engagement with the Holy Spirit's leading.

Finding our spiritual direction

All the above may have whetted your appetite to look for a spiritual director, or perhaps even to become one yourself. But whether this is so or not, you may be reading this because you are seeking new ways to grow in your faith. Since the Holy Spirit is the ultimate spiritual director, you can trust him to meet you in your desire for Christian growth, and enable you to discover your direction.

Cultivating openness to God is vital. This means being willing to respond to his call in every area of living. Thomas Merton advises that 'the spiritual life is not just the life of the mind, or of the affections, or of the "summit of the soul" – it is the life of the whole person'.[6] Thus every part of our four-fold movement towards deeper connection with God, ourselves, others and our environment falls within its scope: each may involve us in discernment, decision-making and personal change.

We also need to be open to the breadth of resources available to us on our spiritual journey. We worship the Creator of the cosmos, not just the Redeemer of the religiously active. Thus the means that can direct us towards God extend beyond the boundaries of church walls out into his world.

Possible stepping-stones along our spiritual path are wide-ranging: from the daily office to our dreams; from God's Creation in nature to human creativity in art, music and literature; from active service in work to quiet attention to bodily awareness and our breathing. They also include psychological tools, such as the Myers-Briggs Type Indicator® personality inventory.

Psychology and spiritual direction

Society's general rejection of institutional religion has been accompanied by a turning to purely psychological routes of personal development – with psychotherapists perhaps looked to as the priesthood of all non-believers. Yet mental health and spiritual wholeness are inextricably linked. The early twentieth-century psychological analyst Carl Jung noted that among all his patients aged 35 upwards, there was not one whose problem was not ultimately that of finding a religious outlook on life.

And the start of the twenty-first century is seeing a fresh awareness in psychological circles of the positive contribution of religious belief to mental health, based on evidence of greater well-being, self-esteem, happiness and purpose in life, as well as lowered rates of depression, anxiety, psychosis and suicide. Significantly, the core therapeutic factors relate to connection: the security of a trust in God, the sense of social belonging and an internal source of strength through Christ's presence within.[7]

From the Christian's perspective, there may be an appropriate caution about putting psychology on too high a pedestal. Yet the dividing line between our mental and spiritual selves is clearly very delicate – and sometimes only dotted! Insights drawn from a psychological source will need to be prayerfully examined and relevantly applied to our spiritual life, but it is immature religion that rejects opportunities for gaining fruitful self-knowledge, preferring to risk the dangers of self-delusion rather than seeking to be led into all truth.

Paul does not urge Christians to discard their understanding, but to be transformed by the renewal of their minds as they grow in spiritual discernment. Psychology can contribute to this process through opening up greater self-awareness and understanding of others in its focus on the deep-seated, sometimes unconscious, tendencies underlying our characteristic patterns of behaviour.

When the Psalmist prayerfully invites God to search and know him in Psalm 139.23, he desires the resulting knowledge to direct him towards greater holiness and a deeper relationship with God. Such an aim distinguishes the faith journey from its psychological counterpart, which may be more concerned with self-actualization and separation than self-giving and God-connectedness. But while mere psychological exploration could lead to an introspective self-indulgence, the faith journey that ignores a psychological element could lead to insensitivity through unawareness. As the Christian writer Anne Long observes, there are 'clear links between psychological and spiritual progress if mature integration is to happen'.[8]

Of course, it is as possible to become a saint without studying psychology as it is to eat healthily without a formal qualification in biochemistry. But, wisely applied, a resource that aids our self-understanding can open up fruitful personal pathways towards our common goal of wholeness in Christ. As Charles Keating puts it, 'God calls us. Knowing ourselves helps us hear him.'[9]

The Myers-Briggs model and spiritual direction

For many Christians, knowing something of the background and pedigree of a model of understanding is an important factor in their decision to use it.

Katherine Briggs and Isabel Myers, the American mother and daughter who originated the Myers-Briggs Type Indicator model, would not lay claim to any specifically Christian credentials. And though academically inclined and able-minded, they did not start out as trained psychologists. The story of the development of what has become the most widely used psychological instrument worldwide is in itself one of faith and achievement over and above the odds.

Katherine Briggs was an inveterate people-watcher and reader of biographies. Based on her observations, she started to formulate categories to discriminate between different personality types. She passed her understanding on to her daughter, Isabel, born in 1897 and educated at home. When Carl Jung's *Psychological Types* was published in English in 1923, Katherine discovered that Jung's theoretical model of personality types crystallized and clarified her own insights. She redirected her studying with new vigour, subsequently corresponding with Jung on type matters.

Things might have ended there, had it not been for America's involvement in the Second World War. Isabel, now married to Clarence Myers, saw how wartime circumstances resulted in women being conscripted into jobs for which they were untrained, inexperienced and often markedly unsuited. Against this backdrop, she and her mother realized the potential value of a knowledge of personality types: to facilitate mutual understanding, better communication and reconciliation, and to enable people to use their particular gifts for others' benefit and their own fulfilment.

With this in mind, the two women became determined to pioneer a way of making their Jungian-based understanding of personality type accessible to all. This became Isabel's passionate vocation. It involved her in over twenty further years of research, acquiring the necessary psychological knowledge and statistical skills on the way, as she developed, tested and validated the assessment questionnaire now known as the Myers-Briggs Personality Type Indicator. She worked painstakingly on her core type textbook *Gifts Differing*[10] for many years, completing it shortly before her death in 1980.

The Myers-Briggs model has been applied to areas of work and personal relationships, education, individual development and counselling and, last but not least, to aspects of spirituality: in the original preface to her book, Isabel Myers included clergy among those 'concerned with the realization of human potential', whom she hoped her book would benefit.

The personal pathway

As Christians we share basic building blocks on our faith journey: Bible reading, prayer, worship and fellowship, applying Jesus' words to our work, personal relationships and the spending of our money, time and energy. Our aim is to be conformed to the *character* of Christ, yet this does not mean adopting a single, identikit *personality*. As Leslie Francis observes, our *character* comprises what develops as the fruit of qualities cultivated by the decisions we make – qualities which might be good or bad; our *personality* is the particular constellation of 'basic, individual differences' at the heart of how we have been made.[11] Since the Bible affirms the uniqueness of each human being, from our physical fingerprint to our psychological imprint, it follows that we each have a distinct personal spiritual path, with our own patterns of relating, gifts, challenges, blind spots, growing edges and places of refreshment. Gaining deeper insight into who we are and how we tick can help put us on track on our particular route to glory, and spare us some spiritual detours and dead-ends. Charles Keating comments on our potential frustration and confusion for us as Christians that can arise when we seek God 'in a manner that he did not create for us'.[12]

Knowing who we are has implications for how we make *all* our connections, with God, others, ourselves and our environment. For, as Richard Rohr observes, 'Everything belongs: How we relate to one area in life is how we relate to all.'[13]

Though individuals, we are called to belong to the body of believers, accountable to each other and needing each other's gifts, companionship, insight and support. Here, an understanding of personality type can deepen our appreciation of others' contributions and defuse some tensions, by shedding light on how we may be interpreting others as difficult when they are simply being different. It may also suggest more effective ways of communicating with those whose natural wavelength differs from ours. If we are involved in spiritual direction at some level, it becomes especially important to be aware of our own assumptions, and open to seeing avenues of growth appropriate for Christians different from ourselves.

Knowledge of our personality type may also bring an awareness of how we habitually regard and respond to our environment, an increasingly pertinent issue for twenty-first-century Christians. The following chapters will introduce Myers-Briggs type theory and help us find our place on the personality type map. We will look at some of the challenges and opportunities our own type faces in connecting with God, others, ourselves and our environment on our particular pathway towards wholeness in Christ. We will consider ways of developing different aspects of our personalities to foster growth, balance and integration. Finally, we will look at the potentials and pitfalls of using the MBTI® instrument on our Christian journey, including the interactions of spiritual direction.

The MBTI rationale is an affirming one: it delineates different but equally valuable personality types, each with their own contribution to make. However, when it comes to finding our spiritual direction, it is a working tool, not a magic wand. As we shall see, it may help us define aspects of our personality, but it will not prescribe a formula or dictate an approach. As our lives have different contexts, circumstances, choices and opportunities, we will still need discernment to decide how best to apply its insights for our own Christian journey. This book is about finding your spiritual direction *with* Myers and Briggs, not *through* them.

2

*Explaining the Myers-Briggs®
model and personality typing*

The prospect of discovering one's personality type raises a range of expectations, from excitement and anxiety through to curiosity, scepticism or plain lack of interest – just as one would expect from our different personalities, backgrounds, approaches and outlooks! Some fear that weaknesses or defects will be exposed and judged as wanting against some acceptable scale of 'normality'. Others resist any notion of being defined by labels and limits. It's therefore important to understand at the outset some principles underlying the Myers-Briggs Type Indicator® model and what it actually measures.

Preferences

We all have preferences, whether we're choosing between coffee or tea, blue or yellow, romance or thriller, city or village, coat or jacket. Some of us are early birds, up with the lark and at our best before breakfast; others are late-nighters, the owls who become live wires after midnight. Choices around how we personally function best may reflect the way we naturally seem to have been put together. There is no value-judgement attached to such tendencies. It's simply part of the glorious diversity of humanity.

Sometimes we can select from a range of options; on other occasions we are more limited. We do not have an endless choice about which hand to write with, for example. It's either left or right.

The Myers-Briggs Type Indicator model identifies four key aspects of living where we exercise a preference in our approach, by choosing between two alternatives. These are:

- where we direct attention and gain energy – Extravert or Introvert;

- how we take in information – Sensing or iNtuition;
- how we make decisions – Thinking or Feeling;
- how we engage with the outer world – Judging or Perceiving.

The various permutations possible in a series of four choices exercised between two alternatives each time result in a total of 16 possible personality 'profiles'. Each of these is characterized by a distinctive approach, perspective and suite of gifts. No type can be classified as superior to another, just as green is not superior to blue – it's just different.

Right hand or left hand?

Before we explore the Myers-Briggs preferences in detail, it may help to do a simple 'handedness' exercise to illustrate and clarify some underlying principles.

Take a blank piece of paper and, on it, sign your name. Below this, sign your name again, only this time, use the pen in your other hand.

How did you experience the contrast between writing the two signatures? What was it like to write with your other hand?

Reflecting on this exercise highlights some key aspects about preferences.

First, when asked to sign your name, you are unlikely to have agonized long and hard over which hand to use. You picked your pen up without hesitation or deliberate thought.

(My mother tells me she knew I would be left-handed from the day I used that hand to grab the spoon she held out to me as an infant. My inborn preference was as normal for me as it would be for another small child to grab a spoon with the right hand.)

Second, consider the contrast between writing with the hand that represents years of choice and experience, and your less-preferred one. Words that people doing this exercise have used to describe the second signing include:

Clumsy	Fun
Awkward	Slow
Childish	Exacting
Incompetent	Illegible

Perhaps you might add some further ones of your own.

When we use our preferred approach to doing things, we are operating in line with an inborn tendency to be, think or act in a certain way. We find the process comes naturally and easily. This predisposes us to choose that approach regularly, and so we build up competence and confidence in that area through our experience. Our preferences develop as we give them attention and cultivate them.

When we opt to tackle something using our less-preferred approach, we feel out of kilter. The activity takes more deliberate effort, and we may perform it more laboriously. We are less likely to be pleased with the quality of the results. This then discourages us from relying on this approach again. As a result, our less-preferred aspects are not able to grow to their full potential – though that would change if we *were* to invest time and energy in developing our skills in those areas.

A final link between our handedness exercise and Myers-Briggs preferences concerns preference strength. Though a left-hander, I still opt to do some things, such as playing racquet sports (after a fashion!), right-handed. But my left-handed friend Claire cannot lead with her right hand in any task. My preference for left-handedness is not as strong as Claire's.

Myers-Briggs personality type theory suggests that this physiological lie of the land has its psychological parallel. In other words:

- Our preferences are inborn.
- Using our preferences is natural. It brings a sense of going with the flow.
- Using our less-preferred aspects is demanding. It brings a sense of going against the grain.
- Our preferences are a measure of our personal choices, not our standards of achievement.
- However, we do tend to develop skills linked to our preferences, as we naturally engage with that approach.
- We can develop skills linked to our less-preferred side, if willing to make the extra effort involved.
- Personality preference strengths can vary.
- Our less-preferred approach may harbour an element of discovery or play.

Bearing this in mind, we will now look at our personality preferences in detail. On the way, you will be invited to assess your own

Attitude	Functions		Attitude
Energy: outside or inside?	*Perceiving*	*Judging*	*Outer lifestyle*
Extravert or Introvert	Sensing or iNtuition	Thinking or Feeling	Judging or Perceiving

Figure 1 The preference-pairs

preferences to build up a profile of your particular Myers-Briggs personality type. Although this will help you come to a useful working understanding, if you seek a more firm grounding in the MBTI® instrument attending a workshop with a qualified MBTI practitioner is highly recommended.[1] This can enable you to:

- take the official MBTI Questionnaire;
- ask your particular questions directly;
- enrich your understanding by interacting with other 'types' in the group.

We have already established that the MBTI model comprises four pairs of alternative preferences, covering four aspects of everyday living. Each preference is indicated by a letter, as indicated in Figure 1.

You can see that the four preference-pairs are organized with the central letters denoting what Myers and Briggs call functions, while the outer letters denote attitudes. (You will also see that the letter for iNtuition is N rather than I. This is because I has already been used for the Introvert preference.)

In exploring the preferences, we will take the central function letters first.

Functions

Our functions are mental processes basic to everyday living: gathering information and deciding how to act in response. We all need to absorb knowledge of our surroundings, and make decisions in the light of this input. In Myers-Briggs terminology, these two processes are known as our functions. In each case, we have a preferred approach to exercising these functions, choosing between two alternatives.

Information-gathering is a passive and receptive process. It is a *Perceiving* function and denoted by the letter S or N.

Making decisions is an active and initiating process. It is a *Judging* function and is denoted by the letter T or F.

Specifics or big picture: Sensing or iNtuition?

When it comes to gathering information, some of us depend consciously on our senses to observe the specifics of our surroundings. Others allow unconscious receptivity to the big picture to 'see' patterns, possibilities and connections not directly discernible by the senses. In Myers-Briggs terminology, this is the difference between exercising a preference for Sensing or iNtuition.

Sensing

Those with a Sensing preference tend to:

- rely on the evidence of what they can see, hear, taste, touch and smell;
- live in the reality of the present moment, experienced through their senses;
- tackle tasks in a methodical, step-by-step manner;
- be attentive and accurate in the details of a task.

People with a developed Sensing preference are very attuned to the physical world around them, and enjoy dealing with established facts. They are precise in following instructions, giving directions, filling in forms and cooking a meal *exactly* according to the recipe. They are at home with practical tasks that require common sense. Because they trust what they can measure, they tend to rely on tried and tested ways of doing things built up through past experience. Sensing tends to be realistic.

iNtuition

Those with an iNtuition preference tend to:

- rely on inspiration and insights emerging from their unconscious;
- live in the potential of future possibilities, envisioned through their unconscious;
- tackle tasks in bursts of enthusiasm, in spontaneous leaps of thought;
- miss the immediate details in their focus on the big picture.

Table 1 Sensing and iNtuition in worship and at prayer

Sensing	iNtuition
Enjoy worship using all the senses: Creation prompts praise.	Enjoy worship that stimulates the imagination: new insight brings wonder.
Prefer known patterns of worship; detailed, specific language and a step-by-step approach.	Prefer changes and new angles in worship; symbolic and image-rich language and an exploratory approach.
Prayer addresses real situations in factual detail. It may use sensing stimuli, such as candles or a natural object.	Prayer connects to underlying meanings with a broad perspective. It may use creative stimuli, such as poetry or music.
Prayer is focused on the present: what is seen is a basis for trusting the promise of eternity.	Prayer looks to future possibilities: what is envisioned catches up current reality in its wake.

People with a developed iNtuition preference are very attuned to the patterns, meanings and potential hidden in what is materially in front of them. They enjoy dealing with new possibilities. They are inspirational in designing a make-over, finding a new route home, understanding abstract concepts and envisioning new projects. They prefer speculative activities that involve imagination. Because they look through and around physical reality, they tend to seek different and inventive ways of doing things, oriented towards a future outcome. iNtuition tends to be idealistic.

Table 1 shows the effect of these preferences in worship and prayer.

Clearly we need to exercise both preferences in order to live effectively: we need to deal with physical reality around us to *manage* our lives; we need to deal with new horizons and unseen elements beyond our material surroundings to *move on* in our lives.

However, Myers-Briggs theory asserts that one of these approaches sits more easily with us.

Take a moment to consider which of these **Perceiving** functions you identify with more closely, so you can allocate yourself a Myers-Briggs letter of S for Sensing or N for iNtuition. Make your choice as far as possible based on what you personally prefer and most naturally do, free of all outer constraints of work or others' expectations.

On your piece of paper, draw a set of four square boxes in a row, and fill in the letter indicating your preference for **S** or **N** in the second box from the left, as indicated below.

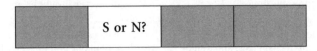

How hard or easy was it to decide, on a scale from 1 (hard) to 5 (easy)? You might like to indicate this by putting the appropriate number below your S/N box, or drawing out a line like the one below, and circling your number on it:

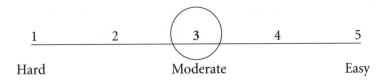

| 1 | 2 | 3 | 4 | 5 |
| Hard | | Moderate | | Easy |

Logical implications or impact on people: Thinking or Feeling?

When we have taken in information, we use it as a basis for making decisions. Some of us approach this process by stepping back to weigh up the factors impersonally and logically; others prefer to remain involved by considering the issues from a personal, relational standpoint. In Myers-Briggs terminology, this is the difference between exercising a preference for Thinking or Feeling. It does not imply that those who prefer Thinking lack emotions, or that those who prefer Feeling lack intelligence. Both processes operate within a rational framework.

Thinking

Those with a Thinking preference tend to:

- organize information according to logical principles and 'cause and effect';
- seek to make decisions that are fair, true and consistent;
- be mindful of the long-term consequences of their decisions;
- address the issue and then attend to the relationship.

People with a developed Thinking preference focus mainly on objective principles and impersonal factors in taking action, regardless of personal feelings. This enables them to make tough, just decisions that have people's better interests at heart, even if this is unappreciated at the time: for example, they will buy a house as a good investment. They can deal with criticism constructively, and tend to voice criticism in order to improve things. They focus on analysing plans.

Feeling

Those with a Feeling preference tend to:

- organize information according to personal interrelationships and values;
- seek to make decisions that are humane, empathetic and harmonious;
- be mindful of the personal impact of their decisions;
- attend to the relationship and then address the issue.

People with a developed Feeling preference focus primarily on subjective values and personal factors, taking action irrespective of logical considerations. This enables them to make kind, merciful decisions that engage people's goodwill and promote unity, even if this seems inconsistent from an objective standpoint: for example, they will buy a home as a welcoming refuge. They take criticism personally, and tend to express appreciation in order to encourage others. They focus on understanding people.

Table 2 shows the effect of these preferences in worship and prayer.

Table 2 Thinking and Feeling in worship and at prayer

Thinking	Feeling
Worship needs challenging content: may appreciate an opportunity to ask questions and discuss theologically.	Worship needs meaningful contact: may appreciate an opportunity to share with others and relate personally.
Prayer is logical, considered and clear-thinking.	Prayer is relational, engaged and open-hearted.
Prayer involves thinking and faces complexity. It focuses on truth and its outworking in pursuing justice in the wider world.	Prayer involves feeling and touches intimacy. It focuses on love and its outpouring in offering service to the wider community.
Faith is guided by universal principles.	Faith is guided by personal values.

Clearly, we need to use both preferences in order to live effectively: we need to make wise, just decisions on principles that hold true however we feel, and we need to exercise care for others and foster harmony and co-operation in our relationships. However, one of these approaches comes more naturally to us.

Consider which of these *Judging* functions you identify with more closely and allocate yourself a Myers-Briggs letter of **T** for Thinking or **F** for Feeling. As before, choose as far as possible based on what you personally prefer and most naturally do, free of all outer constraints of work or others' expectations.

Using the set of boxes you have drawn, fill in the letter indicating your preference for **T** or **F** in the third box from the left.

These central letters are your two preferred Myers-Briggs functions.

How hard or easy was it to decide, on a scale from 1 (hard) to 5 (easy)? Add the appropriate number below your box, or draw a numbered line (as shown for **S/N**) and circle your chosen number.

Attitudes

All of us live in the outer world, acting and interacting with what is around us, and in our inner world of thoughts and emotions. The MBTI instrument refers to these two orientations as attitudes. We have a preferred approach to how we like to operate in these worlds, and which we find more energizing.

Joy of closure or joy of process: Judging or Perceiving?

We all have a lifestyle – our preferred way of operating in our outer world. Some like to go with the flow and keep things open-ended. Such people prefer to use the information-gathering, *Perceiving* function (**S** or **N**) in the outer world.

Some like to organize life and have things sorted. Such people prefer to use the decision-making, *Judging* function (**T** or **F**) in the outer world.

In Myers-Briggs terminology, this is the difference between exercising a Judging or a Perceiving preference. The important point to note here is that the attitude letters **J** or **P** are linked to the function letters we have just considered. They tell us which of the function pairs we most like to use in our outer world.

There is no connotation of being judgemental with the Judging preference. It merely marks an approach that contrasts with its Perceiving counterpart. Whether we prefer **J** or **P** is often the first aspect we notice about each other when we interact, as it concerns our outer world.

Judging

Those with a Judging preference tend to:

- act deliberately, according to a preformed plan;
- be more comfortable once a decision has been made;
- enjoy finishing projects;
- keep focused.

People with a developed Judging preference have an organized approach to life. They like to keep it under control. They make lists, follow plans and meet deadlines with a disciplined schedule. They enjoy the freedom of being able to act according to what they have decided, rather than be swayed by circumstances. They want to know where they are going so they can stay on course. The function they prefer using in their outer world is the *Judging* function of Thinking or Feeling, the function that relates to decision-making.

Perceiving

Those with a Perceiving preference tend to:

- act spontaneously, responding to whatever arises;
- be more comfortable when situations are left open-ended;
- enjoy starting projects;
- remain adaptable.

People with a developed Perceiving preference take a flexible approach to life. They like to go with the flow. They explore new avenues, change direction and meet deadlines in a last-minute rush. They enjoy the freedom of being able to act according to the current situation, rather than being bound by preset plans. They want to keep their options open, so they don't miss out. The function they prefer using in their outer world is the *Perceiving* function

Table 3 Judging and Perceiving in worship and at prayer

Judging	Perceiving
Prefer ordered worship with set liturgy.	Prefer spontaneous worship with space for the unexpected.
Seek an outcome from worship.	Are content with the process of worship.
Prayer is disciplined, and at established times, despite mood or circumstance. May follow a set system or established format.	Prayer is as prompted, at different times, more in line with mood or circumstance. May experiment with or explore different types of prayer.
Organize their devotional life as a spiritual exercise, separate from other activities.	Encounter their devotional life as a spiritual experience, integrated with other aspects of living.

of Sensing or iNtuition, the function that relates to information-gathering.

Table 3 shows the effect of these preferences in worship and prayer.

Clearly, we need to exercise both preferences in order to live effectively: we need to fulfil our responsibilities and manage our lives, and we also need to respond to the needs of the moment.

Consider which attitude you identify with more closely and allocate yourself a Myers-Briggs letter of J for Judging or P for Perceiving. Remember to make your choice as far as possible based on what you personally prefer and most naturally do.

Using the set of boxes you have drawn, fill in the letter indicating your preference for J or P in the fourth box from the left.

How hard or easy was it to decide, on a scale from 1 (hard) to 5 (easy)? Add the appropriate number below your box, or draw a numbered line and circle your chosen number.

Talk it out or think it through: Extravert or Introvert?

Our final preference-pair is another attitude letter.

Though we inhabit both an outer and an inner world, we tend to gain more stimulation from one or the other. The Myers-Briggs terminology for this distinction is the choice between Extraversion and Introversion. These words cover far more than their common modern definition of 'talkative' or 'reserved'.

Extraversion

Those with an Extravert preference tend to:

- be energized by the active outer world of people and things;
- think out loud: like to talk things over;
- become drained by too much time alone;
- have a wide social circle.

People with a developed Extravert preference gain energy for living through contact with others, in doing things and being caught up in the variety and noise of the world around them. They tend to be easy to get to know as they initiate conversation with others and freely express their thoughts and emotions. They move quickly into action, and may only reflect on it later. They are likely to have a broad range of interests and enjoy the variety of stimulation these offer. With an Extraverted preference, what you see is what you get, and you will simply need to listen to find out what they are thinking.

Introversion

Those with an Introvert preference tend to:

- be energized by the reflective inner world of thoughts and feelings;
- think in quiet: like to think things through;
- become drained by too much time with others;
- have a few close friendships.

People with a developed Introvert preference gain energy for living through time spent alone, in reflecting on things and being drawn to the quiet in the world inside them. They tend to be difficult to get to know as they wait to be approached in conversation and reserve disclosing their thoughts and emotions for a select few. They reflect carefully before acting, and may not reach a point of action at all. They are likely to have a narrow range of interests they enjoy pursuing at concentrated depth. With an Introverted preference, there is more than meets the eye, and you will need to ask to find out what they are thinking.

Table 4 Extravert and Introvert in worship and at prayer

Extravert	Introvert
Enjoy participation and action. Like large gatherings.	Enjoy observation and reflection. Like small groups.
Seek self-expression and engagement in worship, e.g. sharing the Peace.	Seek anonymity in worship, e.g. through format of a set liturgy.
Prayer may be out loud and hands-on. Like accessible prayer forms.	Prayer may be silent or in private. Like complex prayer patterns.
Prefer to do and discuss, learn through interaction with others, act and seek God without.	Prefer to reflect and write, learn through reading, contemplate and seek God within.

Table 4 shows the effect of these preferences in worship and prayer.

Clearly, we need to exercise both preferences in order to live effectively: we need to engage with the outside world in our everyday, practical living, and we also need an inner grounding of reflection, focus and self-awareness.

Consider which one of these attitudes you identify with more closely and allocate yourself a Myers-Briggs letter of **E** for Extraversion or **I** for Introversion. Remember to choose as far as possible based on what you personally prefer and most naturally do.

Using the set of boxes you have drawn, fill in the letter indicating your preference for **E** or **I** in the first from the left.

E or I?			

How hard or easy was it to decide, on a scale from 1 (hard) to 5 (easy)? Add the appropriate number below your box, or draw a numbered line and circle your chosen number.

You should now have written all four letters of your self-assessed Myer-Briggs personality profile in your row of four boxes, and have noted down a number score reflecting how easy or hard it was to make each choice.

E or I	S or N	T or F	J or P

Attitude	Functions		Attitude
Energy: outside or inside?	*Perceiving*	*Judging*	**Outer lifestyle**
Extravert *(Talk it out)*	Sensing *(Specifics)*	Thinking *(Logical implications)*	Judging *(Joy of closure)*
or Introvert *(Think it through)*	or iNtuition *(Big picture)*	or Feeling *(Impact on people)*	or Perceiving *(Joy of process)*

Figure 2 Attitudes and functions

This is summed up in Figure 2.

Now turn to the next chapter to find your profile described among the 16 personality types presented.

3

Personality type profiles

———◦•◦———

The MBTI® Type Table in Table 5 is the standard chart for displaying all the personality types, so once you have identified your particular square, you will always know where to find yourself when any type information is presented in this format. The personality profiles that follow are listed in order, going down the Type Table row by row.

Find the profile matching your self-assessment in Chapter 2. Ideally you will recognize yourself straight away. However, if this does not seem quite right, refer to your 1–5 scoring for how hard or easy it was to decide between each preference-pair. Find the lowest number, indicating the hardest choice (and therefore the least clear preference). Swap the corresponding preference letter with its alternative and read the matching profile. So if you assessed yourself as ESTP, but gave yourself a 1 to represent a difficult J/P choice, you might find it helpful to read the ESTJ profile, to see if you identify with it more closely.

Your object is to find your 'best-fit' type. So as you read and reflect on what follows, feel free to take a few personality profiles

Table 5 The MBTI® Type Table

ISTJ	ISFJ	INFJ	INTJ
ISTP	ISFP	INFP	INTP
ESTP	ESFP	ENFP	ENTP
ESTJ	ESFJ	ENFJ	ENTJ

to the fitting room and try them on for size, till you find the most comfortable fit.

ISTJ

Keywords

Painstaking	Logical
Methodical	Practical
Faithful	Responsible
Persistent	Straightforward
Conventional	Decisive

At their best

ISTJs' energy is directed inwards like the quiet intensity of a reference library. ISTJs observe their surroundings with their senses to accumulate a rich, inner store of factual data, which they process and categorize according to their internal framework. Using this knowledge to ascertain what is needed for things to run efficiently, ISTJs then work to achieve this through practical, structured action. Their common sense and capable application of proven procedures ensures their success as administrators or project managers. ISTJs prefer working alone and uninterrupted, accepting responsibility for the end results.

ISTJs possess a keen sense of duty, often carrying more than their fair share of the workload. Efficient, dependable, accurate with detail and patient with routine, they may rise to leadership positions, though their modest, systematic approach to fulfilling obligations means it is usually others who recognize their merits. As pillars of their communities, ISTJs are at home in established institutions, bringing stability through their steady support.

Though they may appear composed and quietly serious, ISTJs' matter-of-fact exterior can conceal a dry wit and original turn of mind, which only emerges in unguarded moments of relaxation with family and friends.

Clear-minded ISTJs respect the facts. While these masters of maintenance are cautious about change, if investigation provides evidence a new procedure will be more effective, they will adopt and hold to it with unshakeable conviction. Pursuit of objectives may also empower ISTJs to overcome their reserve and interact socially, promoting their ideas and expressing emotions. They can don the extravert mantle so convincingly others may not realize how naturally private they are.

How they connect

ISTJs connect through their senses and their service, in the reality of factual observation and tangible engagement.

God for ISTJs is the unseen Creator whose nature is revealed through his ordered, physical universe. Acknowledging his power, ISTJs seek to respond as dutiful servants by obeying his commands and honouring their commitments. ISTJs *meet God* through the testimonies of other Christians' lives, past and present. They encounter him in diligent acts of service and disciplined devotions, building their own experience of God's loving care through his answers to their specific prayers, alone or with one or two trusted others.

ISTJs connect *with others* by seeking to be of use. They show care by taking responsibility: whatever another's shortcomings, ISTJs will step in to help if needed. Unswervingly loyal, they work hard to achieve good relationships and keep promises of commitment. ISTJs speak their minds more easily than their hearts. They feel deeply, but regard faithful action as louder than warm words, and may not be verbally effusive in expressing affection: their practical support and consistent provision are proof of where love lies. ISTJs' logic serves them well with those whose approach makes little sense to them. As they accept others' emotions or idiosyncrasies as facts with which to reckon, ISTJs can bypass their own lack of understanding to act in loving consideration.

ISTJs set great store by their community connections. They are faithful upholders of institutions, from work-place to family and church. Social structures are at least as important to ISTJs as the individuals involved, and ISTJs are generous with their time and energy in maintaining them. ISTJs operate by defining their relationship roles and goals. A clear sense of exactly what is required helps them function more comfortably socially and personally. It also clarifies what to expect – and insist upon – from others.

ISTJs may *see themselves* as simply doing what needs to be done, and so undervalue their contributions to others' lives. Putting duty before all else, they may lose touch with their own inner feelings.

It can be hard for ISTJs to reconnect with their emotions: they may associate such expression with lack of self-control.

ISTJs enjoy orderly *surroundings*. Their homes may be functional and unfussy, tasteful and tidy. In environmental matters, they may seek to be trustworthy stewards of God's Creation. Once persuaded of its tangible benefits, ISTJs are likely to be scrupulous in carrying out any 'green' policy to the letter – as well as ensuring it is followed by all in their sphere of responsibility.

ISFJ

Keywords

Devoted	Modest
Loyal	Practical
Supportive	Gentle
Organized	Precise
Responsible	Traditional

At their best

ISFJs' energy flows inwards as waves of outer information impact on their senses and soak into their psyche like sea-water seeping through sand. They hold impressions of particular significance in safe-keeping within their rich interior storehouse of memories and experiences. ISFJs' keen observation of their surroundings is quietly trained on how other people's behaviour reveals their needs. This focus, plus their care for others' welfare and their orderly approach to life, orientates ISFJs towards attentive service that makes a practical difference, such as in health care or administrative support.

ISFJs' gifts are richly expressed in nurturing or parenting roles. Their approach is characterized by detail, devotion and a determination to finish the job. They are reliable and ready to help wherever they see a need, and most especially among their closest circles of family, friends and work colleagues, where they can respond one-to-one.

ISFJs do not court attention. Their presentation tends to be dutiful rather than dramatic, and others may undervalue or take for granted their acts of service. ISFJs are generally too modest to make a fuss, yet they cherish expressions of appreciation when they receive them. Though they may not push to stand out in a crowd, ISFJs can be highly individual and idiosyncratic in their own personal interests or hobbies. They may pursue these with a surprising degree of passion and dedication, acquiring detailed knowledge and seeking out fellow-enthusiasts. At times, too, they may quietly observe the ways of a world seemingly indifferent to their values and priorities with a twinkle in their eyes.

How they connect

ISFJs connect primarily through their call to serve and need to be needed.

As natural nurturers, ISFJs may *respond to God* as Father, who maintains order and provides care and security for his children. They may also value 'seeing' God through Jesus, the Servant King and Good Shepherd who has made God tangible in his incarnate actions of merciful, practical love for humankind. ISFJs may sense Jesus' presence as they seek to please him by following his example, are enfolded in the quietness of ordered worship, or faithfully mark the recurring seasons of the Christian calendar.

Considerate and courteous, ISFJs find meaning through *affirming others*. They are ready to make sacrifices in serving them if necessary. ISFJs are shy in manner, though their quiet warmth and friendliness emerges as they become more comfortable. They form relationships slowly, but once these are forged, ISFJs offer indefatigable long-term commitment. They work hard to make family occasions memorable and mark special days. ISFJs enjoy belonging and contributing to any established social group where there are clear conventions to follow or rules to obey, such as family, church or other organization, though their focus remains primarily on people rather than institutions. They are likely to join a club that reflects their particular hobby or interest.

ISFJs' commitment to work for others' best interests makes them vulnerable to neglecting their own. They may be exploited by those around them: their desire to co-operate rather than be in control can result in their becoming unduly subservient. ISFJs struggle to deal with relationships that have gone awry, because of the high value they place on personal loyalty. Their sense of responsibility inclines them to hold themselves accountable rather than blame another.

ISFJs' may delay *considering themselves* until they have finished what they feel needs doing for others. They may disregard their own emotional stress, only allowing themselves to rest when physical symptoms of tiredness surface. ISFJs ground their identity in familiar patterns and are unlikely to harbour great ambitions for personal change.

ISFJs have a keen sense of the aesthetics of their personal *surroundings*. They may be highly effective interior designers and decorators. They may feel overwhelmed by the concept and scale of global environmental concerns, if not translated into immediate specific acts of care for Creation they can make in response. A well-tended and attractively ordered garden may appeal to them more than wild mountain grandeur.

INFJ

Keywords

Creative	Individual
Compassionate	Visionary
Complex	Insightful
Authentic	Sensitive
Idealistic	Intense

At their best

INFJs' energy is directed towards an inner flow of ideas, inspirations and intuitions, welling up from within like the bubbling emergence of an underground spring. Their attention tends towards the human arena. This focus, combined with a future-orientation and a natural penchant for the abstract and intangible, may draw them to work in psychological or spiritual fields. Here, their discernment into a person's inner dynamics can penetrate beneath the surface with uncanny accuracy.

INFJs channel their empathy and creativity into others' personal development, as well as engaging in an ongoing quest for authentic wholeness within their own selves. They are idealists with a deep sense of call to offer meaningful service towards the achievement of human potential. Although unlikely to assert leadership, INFJs may 'punch above their weight' when it comes to influencing others, which they do by individual encouragement and quiet inspiration.

The vitality of INFJs' interior world may not always be apparent to those around them, as they are outwardly gentle in manner. Yet their strong sense of inner 'knowing' may sometimes emerge in a surprising determination to hold to their line.

INFJs are captivated by reaching beyond existing patterns to grasp complex new connections and fresh possibilities for people. This faces them with the challenge of communicating their insights, which they may meet with artistic dexterity or fluency in the written word. INFJs are at home with the language of symbol and metaphor as ways of formulating what is as yet inexpressible because it transcends the boundaries of ordinary seeing.

How they connect

INFJs seek to make meaningful connections. Their approach to their key relationships may reflect the intensity and high expectations they apply to themselves.

God for INFJs is mysteriously transcendent, yet deeply personal. They yearn towards an authentic encounter with him that may go beyond words: INFJs are the most natural mystics of all types. They are drawn to the depths to hear the still small voice of God within. They are inspired by the heights as they see the vision of God's Kingdom to come. They may meet him most powerfully in silent space, or through reflective or poetic writing in a personal spiritual journal.

INFJs' longing for harmony with God extends outwards in a desire to *connect peaceably with others*, whom they value as part of the glorious complexity of created humanity. This can make INFJs appear sociable, but they are never truly 'one of the crowd', and will not conform at the cost of their personal integrity. They are sincerely caring though not outwardly effusive, and are hard to genuinely get to know. They tend to hold back their deepest thoughts and most profound feelings, sharing these only with their inmost circle. Yet expressing themselves and exploring their insights with those they trust is a vital and valuable process for INFJs. It helps them clarify their thoughts and communicate them to the outer world.

One reason for INFJs' reserve may be their acute sensitivity – a facet of their quality of empathy. INFJs can be easily hurt. If demoralized by criticism or crushed by conflict, they may withdraw or become extremely stubborn to protect themselves and secure the space they need to reflect and recover. Their behaviour may sometimes appear contradictory, as they move from apparent acquiescence in company to abruptly cutting others off and retiring into their own world. Since INFJs' driving force is located inside, there may be few outer clues to what has prompted this seemingly random shift.

INFJs have a keen level of psychological and spiritual *self-awareness*, and a pressing desire to achieve their full personal potential. This includes achieving the optimum in their closest relationships, even if they cannot offer a precise definition of their ideals.

INFJs tend to relate to the *wider environment* in abstract and even symbolic terms, rather than via immediate experience. They may, for example, be more acutely concerned about global warming and its future impact on people, than observant of the day-to-day details of their own back garden.

INTJ

Keywords

Independent	Challenging
Analytical	Global
Visionary	Theoretical
Determined	Detached
Inventive	Efficient

At their best

INTJs' energy flashes inwardly in bursts of insight like lightning revealing the shape of an unseen landscape. Their intuition discerns patterns, meanings and connections, and generates ideas and inspirations. INTJs analyse these creatively, formulating new solutions to satisfy their ongoing quest to improve everything around them. They shape their insights into systems that make them accessible to the outside world. INTJs' gifts flourish where they face stimulating challenges, and can work autonomously to pursue discoveries and innovative practices that move society towards a better future.

INTJs can absorb and understand complex issues in global terms. This, along with their decisiveness as pioneers of new pathways, may lead them to achieve responsible positions within organizations. INTJs are also strongly independent individualists: competence, rather than conformity, is their goal. Their incisive thinking is unconstrained by the status quo, piercing through conventional wisdom to view things from an imaginative angle, beyond established forms of thought. Self-possessed and confident, INTJs trust their own insight and competence.

INTJs' intellectual clarity can carry an aura of entrenched elitism. In truth, their continual search for deeper understanding means they are open to challenge. INTJs can be flexible in changing their position if convinced by a cogent argument for a better alternative.

INTJs have an intense drive to implement their ideas, and work towards this end with single-minded persistence and concentration. It is not enough to synthesize theory: it needs to be systemized into practice. Verbally articulate, INTJs communicate their strategies with economy, elegance and subtlety, though are unlikely to disclose the full riches of their inner reasoning.

How they connect

INTJs connect through their minds, in deep-thinking, wide-ranging ways and taking an objective and dispassionate stance.

INTJs *see God* as the touchstone of truth, justice and holiness. Their global perspective envisions him as the source of endless possibilities for transformation across the interconnected cosmos, the one in whom all things hold together. INTJs meet him as they surrender their capabilities and independent wills to his lordship. They dialogue with God in private theological reflection, seeking to discern his truth and apply its implications intelligently and consistently to their lives. They may also exhort the Church to worship in spirit and truth, by changing its traditions where necessary.

INTJs' intellects stimulate and are stimulated by *those around them*. They prefer debating theory to passing the time of day, and connect most easily to those who share their appetite for exploration and challenge. What INTJs experience as amicable interaction, others may find argumentative. INTJs' logical approach harbours an expectation that people will function rationally. Intelligent application of their intuition, rather than natural emotional attunement, helps them understand others, and they prefer resolving issues through reasoned discussion rather than offering emotional support. INTJs may analyse a relationship's requirements objectively, develop their own ideal model, and then behave accordingly.

Independent and self-contained, INTJs take time to develop close relationships, but once intimacy is forged, they value the security it brings. They respond with trust, revealing the sense of fun, responsiveness to love and sensitivity to rejection beneath their reserve. INTJs' devotion may emerge less in demonstrative emotion – for them, integrity means more than sentimentality – than in a passionate commitment to mutual growth. INTJs work hard to better their relationships, demanding much of themselves as well as others. They will address issues with robust directness and truth, communicate clearly and listen fairly. INTJs respect others' competence, allowing them room to grow without being smothered.

INTJs *connect with themselves* through the vitality of their inner world, envisioning and analysing possibilities to determine their own unique path. The fruit of such introspection is a profound certainty of their own rightness. They may become frustrated if their ideals are undermined by reality.

Organized INTJs prefer tidy physical *surroundings*, though may not particularly notice them if absorbed by a current project. Their global perspective enables them to grasp the complexities of large-scale environmental issues, and their ability to use knowledge and understanding to 'think outside the box' may well yield the alternative solutions and long-range strategies needed for a future-conscious stewardship of the planet.

ISTP

Keywords

Practical	Observant
Reserved	Spontaneous
Logical	Autonomous
Adaptable	Expedient
Direct	Adventurous

At their best

ISTPs' energy is directed inwards like the continuous momentum of an active computer program. Using their five senses to register factual details about things around them, ISTPs analyse the information gleaned to discern underlying principles and problems. They respond with immediate practical action to provide expedient solutions. Though able in many areas, ISTPs' relish for exploring what makes things tick means they thrive best where they can work independently to understand, bring to order, fix or improve things, perhaps in mechanical, technological or statistical fields.

Earthy ISTPs learn through hands-on exploration and laid-back observation. They continuously monitor their environment, accumulating an encyclopaedic store of information. This reservoir of knowledge readies them for cool, efficient action at all times, and their deft response in a crisis may seem almost instinctive. ISTPs value economy of effort. They seek the most direct route to tangible results, without wasting energy on emotional flurry, reading instructions, following rules or making plans.

ISTPs' outer reserve reveals little of their inner responsiveness to surroundings. But when something captures their interest, detached ISTPs may suddenly involve themselves enthusiastically in a task. This unpredictable behaviour gives them an enigmatic aura. Free-spirited ISTPs seek the stimulation of fresh experiences, risk-taking challenges and constant action. Their fearlessness, alert physical awareness and co-ordination make them adept at sports and outdoor activities. They may also excel as artisans or craftspeople, displaying dexterity and precision as masters of their tools. ISTPs may have a unique range of interests, and can be single-minded in pursuit of their own personal projects.

How they connect

ISTPs connect via their senses, finding their place in the world and their own aliveness through engaging with physical reality around them.

God for ISTPs is a God of action, whose incarnate Son undertook the ultimate challenge of the journey to the Cross, thus affirming and redeeming physical Creation. Direct and straightforward in their faith, ISTPs eschew religious structures and theological complexities to follow the Master in principled, practical service. They meet God in spontaneous moments, as they practise his presence in the daily round. Prayer happens on the job, as ISTPs seek to know God alongside them in their work.

ISTPs connect most directly *with others* through shared activities. In active mode, ISTPs' bright and exciting presence makes them fun, if unpredictable, as companions. In observer mode, they become self-contained, asking more questions than they will answer, and testing the water before expressing a personal view. Though ISTPs enjoy company, they may resist pressure to conform to expectations of sociability: independent-minded ISTPs stand apart from the crowd as much by choice as by accident. They need time alone to process their thoughts, but their strong belief in an individual's right to personal space means they allow others the same freedom. ISTPs' apparent shyness disappears when the conversation turns to their own particular interests.

ISTPs value fairness and loyalty, but their strong attunement to the present moment means they live out their personal relationship commitments one day at a time. They express care generously, through deeds or gestures rather than words. Generally tolerant of others, ISTPs build a strong network of relationships that meet their uncomplicated needs. They also look to their relationships for new experiences – even if that means injecting some excitement into the mix themselves. Though ISTPs can feel intensely, their uncertainty in the emotional arena may make them reticent about revealing their own feelings, or becoming uncomfortably entangled in those of others.

ISTPs gain a sense of *themselves* through tactile contact with the outer world, which fosters awareness of their own reality. They are conscious of their inner world of thoughts and impersonal reason, but pay less attention to their feelings, and may even distrust them. ISTPs' precise observation and immediate physical interaction with their *surroundings* can result in a deep experience of oneness with their environment. Their sensitivity to beauty enables them both to create it and to appreciate it. Long-term environmental issues may seem at one remove, but ISTPs are up for any worthwhile 'green' activity, the more adventurous and physically challenging the better.

ISFP

Keywords

Gentle	Creative
Adaptable	Modest
Compassionate	Observant
Sensitive	Loyal
Reflective	Harmonious

At their best

ISFPs' energy glows like a kiln's heat: with outer warmth, but inner incandescence. ISFPs' senses are finely tuned to observe details of the world around them with fresh, uncomplicated vision. Assimilating what they absorb in accordance with a deeply felt call to encourage wholeness in all living beings, ISFPs respond in practical actions that nurture healing and harmony. They thrive in serving others through hands-on care to meet immediate needs, with freedom to be versatile and creative as circumstances demand, possibly in medical, veterinary or educational fields.

Action-oriented and free-spirited ISFPs appreciate life fully, moment by precious moment. They evince a quiet sense of delight and discovery as they take time to savour their surroundings and express tender care for all they meet – ISFPs are highly sensitive to others' feelings, with a great capacity for love and understanding. Though they eschew routine for spontaneity, their journey through life is neither haphazard nor indecisive, but guided by inner ideals they do not necessarily articulate.

Though ISFPs may appear carefree and serene, they take life seriously, and are devoted to others' welfare through intense personal conviction. If their values are threatened, these gentle individuals may adopt a surprisingly firm stance, often on others' behalf.

ISFPs' practical creativity includes inanimate as well as living things. Their discerning eye and physical dexterity may lead them to become gifted and graceful artists, whose eloquence is expressed in their hands rather than through their words. Their bodily awareness and quick reactions may also bring sporting prowess. Though naturally self-effacing, dedicated ISFPs may display greatness as aesthetes or athletes.

How they connect

ISFPs' receptivity and responsiveness to all life around them in the here and now gives them a profound sense of connectedness.

ISFPs discern God's artistic hand and loving heart through every aspect of Creation. Their natural spiritual awareness means ISFPs are not confined to *meeting God* at set times and places, but respond to him in grateful spontaneous prayer and praise wherever they happen to be. Their holistic engagement with God may emerge through prayer involving physical expression from posture to dance, creativity in music or art, and practically in unplanned acts of kindness prompted by the Holy Spirit.

Though ISFPs more easily *connect with others* most sympathetic to their way of being, their affirming outlook enables them to see something positive in every individual, and their open-minded sympathy can embrace those on the margins. Easygoing rather than outgoing, ISFPs prefer listening to talking, making them easy to like but harder to know. They may elude understanding as they chart a quietly original course, in their undemanding, low-key style. ISFPs respect others' freedom, generously offering them the space and grace so vital for their own growth. However, their tendency to defer to others' needs rather than assert their own makes them vulnerable to others riding roughshod over their tolerant docility.

Kind-hearted ISFPs are easily hurt by conflict, and may use reserve as self-protection when they feel under threat, rather than risk confrontation. They may take time to develop intimate relationships and fully reveal their sensitivity and playfulness, but once established, ISFPs' closest bonds receive their deepest love and loyalty, with any number of thoughtful, imaginative gifts and gestures offered as markers of affection. ISFPs also need to be appreciated and, more importantly, encouraged to value themselves, as they tend to underrate their gifts. They may enjoy a special connection with children and animals, where heartfelt links are made beyond words, and love is returned unconditionally.

ISFPs' combination of sensual alertness and inner reflection leads to keen *self-awareness*. Their joy in life may be shaken by burdening feelings of inadequacy when they perceive the gap between their desire for harmony and the limitations of their circumstances.

ISFPs are attentive to the details of their immediate *surroundings*, and seek to create beauty and harmony around them. Their homes are likely to be attractive, artistic and possibly filled with plants and pets: ISFPs cherish the natural world and all God's creatures. Deep environmental concern may inspire them to adopt causes from pacifism to vegetarianism.

INFP

Keywords

Adaptable	Curious
Compassionate	Empathic
Creative	Humble
Devoted	Peaceable
Contemplative	Altruistic

At their best

INFPs' energy is directed inwards towards deeply held values that cherish humanity, like the self-contained warmth of a fur-lined coat. The outworking of these core personal values is defined and refined in the light of INFPs' insightful perception of possibilities in the lives of those around them. INFPs feel a vocation to make the world a better place. Their quest for purpose in life finds fulfilment in serving others through occupations that foster personal growth and social good, and allow them some leeway to express their compassion creatively.

INFPs are congenial and adaptable. Though not flamboyantly emotional, they quietly exude affection and empathy, as they listen to and validate others' feelings, needs, hopes and dreams. They are fascinated explorers of the complexities of personality and questions of identity, including their own. But underneath a tranquil exterior and easygoing acceptance, INFPs are demanding of themselves. Idealists and perfectionists, they pursue their self-determined goals with all-consuming devotion, whatever the self-sacrifice involved.

INFPs' inner convictions are as passionate as they are outwardly invisible. However, that can change abruptly: if a cherished value is violated or a personal cause dismissed, these peaceable individuals may react with volcanic fervour and ferocity.

INFPs' yearning for the ideal that transcends the limitations of the real may find an outlet in imaginative artistic expression. INFPs need individual space to dream, reflect and formulate their deepest insights. Their self-effacing nature that eschews the limelight, yet longs to communicate, may be best satisfied by writing in the quietness of a study, rather than speaking in the cut and thrust of the market-place.

How they connect

INFPs connect via their hearts, unobtrusively, but intensely and personally, and with their characteristic vision of perfection.

For INFPs, *God* is Love, the source of perfect compassion, endless mystery, author of a wonderfully diverse Creation, that is forever unfolding yet ultimately enfolded in grace. INFPs are drawn to forge an authentic personal connection with the One before whom they can be truly themselves, to experience deep communion in a relationship with endless potential for growth. They may intuitively sense God's presence and love, meeting him through individual prayer of every kind: from heartfelt expressions of devotion to deep contemplation.

As INFPs reach out to make meaningful *connections with others*, their good humour, responsiveness and emotional sensitivity mean they get along well with most. They enjoy pleasing others and drawing out their potential. While they seek authenticity and harmony in their relationships, INFPs only reveal their inmost hearts to their trusted circle of intimates, to whom they are intensely loyal and devoted. Even here, the depth of INFPs' inner tenderness may not be fully expressed outwardly. INFPs have no drive to impress or impose. This may mean their attentiveness towards others is unreciprocated, and their own needs for affirmation unmet. INFPs may take time forming their closest relationships, as they may have highly romantic expectations.

INFPs can be effective group catalysts and mediators, though they abhor personal conflict and will avoid it wherever possible: they feel criticism intensely, and may blame themselves for interpersonal stress around them. However, INFPs are individualistic, and enjoy an originality of approach. Rather than accomplish this through head-on confrontation, these gentle individualists will find a more subtle way: like water finding the cracks in a system, their uniqueness flows through structures, quietly subverting others' labels and definitions of them.

INFPs relate to *themselves* with profound, but sometimes unsettled, self-awareness. They continually question their role and identity, despite their underlying self-reliance. Their sense of a mismatch between their aspirations and actual achievements may lead to self-criticism. Responsive to the complex and the beautiful, INFPs may cherish Creation as God's personal artistic expression, worthy of wonder. Their future-oriented focus and global perspective may fuel an idealistic longing to protect and cherish the *environment*. INFPs may find breaking down this long-term goal into small practical steps brings dismay, as such actions seem an inadequate response to the overwhelming nature of the task.

INTP

Keywords

Self-contained	Profound
Independent	Reserved
Original	Precise
Theoretical	Sceptical
Analytical	Logical

At their best

INTPs' energy flows inwards in a quest for truth, following pathways of abstract thought with all the intricacies of a labyrinth journey. Their intuition scans the world, discerning patterns, problems and possibilities. INTPs then analyse their accumulating store of knowledge logically to crystallize underlying principles and formulate ingenious new approaches. Their intellectual creativity and curiosity thrive in occupations from technology to theology, where they can work flexibly as independent-minded architects, researching and designing systems without having to effect their practical application.

INTPs exercise intense concentration as they work alone on complex concepts. They are patient problem-solvers, developing constructs that penetrate to the root of the issue, their thinking unconstrained by accepted assumptions. Their original solutions may pioneer breakthroughs to new ground. Yet INTPs view all conclusions as provisional. Captivated by the task of completing a coherent picture even as new pieces emerge, INTPs continually dismantle and refine their theories to bring them ever closer to perfection.

Generally undemanding and content with a simple lifestyle, INTPs can appear easygoing. Yet underneath this outer placidity, their minds are absorbed in inner activity, pursuing inspirations and organizing ideas as they strive to master the current mental challenge. INTPs insist on communicating their ideas in a way that exactly encapsulates their line of thought: what has been precisely conceived must be appropriately expressed, without compromise for the sake of accessibility. Their determination for insights not to be rendered inaccurate through being generalized or over-simplified fuels INTPs' capacity for elegant distinction in their use of language. At its best, this gives form to visionary perceptions.

How they connect

INTPs connect primarily via their minds, as they engage intellectually in exploration, observation and reflection.

God for INTPs is impersonal, the mysterious unfolding Truth, testing human understanding, and inspiring the ultimate quest: the pursuit of knowledge of the unfathomable depths of the divine. INTPs meet him through study of his word and world, and in encounter with other great minds, as they undertake an open-ended, rational exploration of matters theological and philosophical. In their private devotional life, INTPs may not be too concerned by the narrow divide between their abstract prayer and inner reflective dialogue. They view God's existence as irrespective of their personal spiritual response.

INTPs' lively intellect makes a spontaneous and good-natured connection with like-minded *others* who share their interests. They are animated in conversations that involve discussion, question and argument about ideas, but set little store by the small-talk that oils the wheels of interpersonal relationships. They may prefer to observe objectively rather than participate personally in community gatherings, and may give scant attention to the social niceties, customs or even dress code of the occasion. INTPs value autonomy: they allow others the independent private space they also need for themselves, and harbour no ambition to be in command. Their general willingness to live and let live only evaporates when another violates their core principles.

INTPs may appear cool in outward demeanour, yet passion can break through in their few cherished close relationships. Where INTPs love, they feel deeply and attach faithfully, though may not often express such an obvious given in visible affection or verbal endearment. INTPs are not at home in the arena of emotional expression: they may respond to warmth selectively and on their own terms, and where emotion surfaces in conflict, their awkwardness may show itself in avoidance or an explosive outburst. INTPs' detachment and ability to weather criticism with equanimity can hide a need to be respected for their competence.

INTPs connect *with themselves* as rational beings, inhabiting a rich inner landscape of thought. They know their own minds and trust their own insights. INTPs demand rigorous personal standards of themselves and may be intolerant of their mistakes.

INTPs are not especially sensitive to the details of their *surroundings* – if indeed they register them – unless their environment is the current focus of their work. They may formulate an underlying rationale for preserving the planet as an issue of justice and social responsibility. The practical implications of their cogitations, however, would be for others to carry forward.

ESTP

Keywords

Pragmatic	Direct
Adventurous	Agile
Flexible	Active
Enthusiastic	Fun-loving
Spontaneous	Persuasive

At their best

ESTPs' energy surges outwards into the action of the moment, like a confined animal suddenly released into the open air. With every sense alert to tangible reality, ESTPs rapidly absorb a wealth of factual detail about people and things around them. They analyse this logically to assess what action the situation requires, and do it directly. ESTPs' gifts excel where their no-nonsense realism and resourceful ingenuity is given free rein to initiate practical action that gets things moving, from stage to salesroom, sports-field to roadside.

ESTPs learn by doing. Their acumen cuts through complexities to create straightforward solutions, regardless of established procedures. Restless with routine, ESTPs prefer life at the frontier. They relish taking risks, venturing outside their comfort zone to rely on their wits, common sense and knowledge amassed through experience. ESTPs are energized by emergencies, in which they prove clear-headed, fast-moving and fearless. They like concrete results for their efforts, and may move on to fresh challenges if feedback is not immediately forthcoming.

Outgoing ESTPs may reveal little of the inner motivations behind their behaviour. This can make them difficult to predict. It may seem paradoxical that such accessible personalities can be so hard to read.

ESTPs sparkle with *joie de vivre* as they take hold of all life offers here and now. These live wires are the life and soul of the party, combining an appetite for action and entertainment with a natural panache. ESTPs compete in whatever game is going, and their keen-minded alacrity generally gives them a winning streak. Their entrepreneurial spirit makes them more effective starters than finishers.

How they connect

ESTPs connect through active engagement with everyone and everything around them as they immerse themselves in the present moment.

For ESTPs, *God* is the Creator of a dynamic universe ripe for exploration and enjoyment. Just as the earthly Jesus obeyed his father at the carpenter's bench and on the road, impacting on all he met in his ministry day by day, so ESTPs meet God on the go, more in the market-place than on the mountain-top. Their God-directed work is their prayer, alongside verbal imprecations that are brief, functional and practical. ESTPs also experience God communally in lively, participative praise and worship.

ESTPs are stimulated by interacting *with others*. Good-natured and willing to take people as they find them, they get along with most, though may seek out those with whom they can share adventures. Assertive and gregarious, ESTPs enjoy regaling an audience with lively tales from their vast fund of experiences. They can be entertaining performers at social gatherings, attracting an entourage of supporters and admirers. ESTPs' alertness to details of body language and facial expression gives them a marked accuracy in reading people. They use their perceptions to persuade, motivate and activate others. ESTPs are also able negotiators. Their adaptability and realistic approach ensure success in achieving expedient solutions.

The energy ESTPs bring to their wide social circle can blaze into their closest relationships. As seekers of excitement, ESTPs may reinvigorate a personal relationship via a grand gesture or generous gift if the momentum is slowing. Flamboyant actions speak louder than tender words, and besides, freedom-loving ESTPs are more confident of their ability to charm than to commit. Their ability to adapt their behaviour to harmonize with how others tick does not necessarily signify an emotional connection, and they may need personal encouragement to allay a tendency to be tentative when it comes to intimate relationships and intense feelings.

ESTPs' interaction with others acts as a mirror, reflecting their own image and connecting them *with themselves*. They may be prone to rely on this outer self-definition. ESTPs' natural vigour gives them little patience with inward reflection, and they tend to be undemanding of themselves.

ESTPs are at home in whatever surroundings they find themselves. They appreciate and care for their material possessions, and have an eye for beauty, both man-made and God-created. Long-term environmental considerations may seem unreal to them, but they will be up for any hands-on activity that meets an immediate need, solves a problem, promises enjoyment or poses an exciting physical challenge.

ESFP

Keywords

Generous	Easygoing
Engaging	Communicative
Adaptable	Lively
Playful	Co-operative
Practical	Enthusiastic

At their best

ESFPs are energized by the outward pull towards fresh experiences with all the force of a wave surging towards the shore. Alive through their senses to everything around them here and now, ESFPs radiate enthusiasm for engaging with the world as they find it. Their delight in material realities is undergirded by inner values that focus on people. ESFPs are drawn to any sociable or stimulating activity, especially one with a problem-solving component. They serve others by finding fresh ways through practical difficulties, and offer valuable support through their capability in a crisis.

ESFPs are accurate observers who develop practical skills and knowledge on the job rather than in the classroom: they flourish in the dynamics of interaction with their environment. Engaging and open, these friendly personalities quickly establish rapport and warm hearts. They are performers, bringing out the fun in the party of life; free spirits, who refuse to let the rules cramp their exuberance and creativity.

ESFPs may appear superficial, as their love of variety propels them impulsively from one activity to another. In truth, they are grounded in the present moment, trusting their common sense and experience to equip them for whatever arises, with no need for forward planning. As natural team-players, ESFPs want everyone to be happy: they may prefer being among the group rather than in a position of formal authority. Their positive attitude, tact and personal skills mean they may be enlisted as peace-makers. Here they often prove effective, though may opt to deflect negative feelings with humorous distraction rather than take the bull by the horns.

How they connect

ESFPs connect through all their five senses, responding to the stimulus of everything around them like a sunflower tracking the sun's beams.

ESFPs experience *God* as the wonderfully versatile Creator of a diverse and delightful planet. They see him as active within his world and in the lives of those made in his image. They may meet him through spontaneous, conversational prayer, interceding directly for the particular needs of those whose lives they touch, thanking him for his answers to their requests, and praising him for the glories of Creation they encounter on their way.

ESFPs' engagement with the Creator and his work overflows outwards in a love for his people. ESFPs are easygoing and tend to be *accepting of others*. They may have a particular rapport with children. Their attentiveness to others' appearance and behaviour leads to such accurate discernment that they may seem intuitive at times. They take great pleasure in eliciting positive responses from others, and may adjust their own approach and style to secure these. They may take criticism very personally. ESFPs form relationships easily, communicate directly, captivate effortlessly, and are spontaneously generous in their outpouring of time, energy and possessions to others, without keeping score.

ESFPs nurture their relationships through providing significant tokens of love: a romantic meal, special card or memento. Their companionship is based on such shared experiences, rather than a commonality of ideas, but their total involvement in the present may mean they do not cling on to relationships long term. A past connection can lose its power to hold ESFPs' ongoing commitment. This is not deliberate rejection, but reflects how they live wholeheartedly with what is, not what was or might be.

ESFPs may find it uncomfortable to stop and relate to their *inner selves*. Deeper reflection may bring anxieties, which they tend to tolerate less robustly than other types. Yet where willing to work through their discomfort, clarify their values and commit to priorities, ESFPs will maximize their effectiveness and impact.

ESFPs are particularly environmentally aware. They attend to their *surroundings*, and may express delight in the beauties of nature, from the sight of a single snowdrop to the rustle of autumn leaves. They may exhibit a special connection with animals. ESFPs empathize with the environment and want to express this through practical and immediate acts of stewardship. Developing long-term policies to care for God's world may seem irrelevant to those who hear Creation groaning now.

ENFP

Keywords

Enthusiastic	Spontaneous
Friendly	Expressive

Curious   Perceptive
Encouraging   Versatile
Creative   Independent

At their best

ENFPs' energy courses outwards like sweeping water-rapids, enveloping and refreshing all in their path. Their intuition scans the environment, searching for meaning through discerning patterns, connections and relationships. ENFPs focus attention on people, seeing beyond who they are to what they could become, and using their insight to motivate others in positive directions. Though widely capable, ENFPs flourish where work is fun *and* offers meaningful service, allowing flexibility in generating new ideas *and* involvement with others. Their appetite for variety and challenge may lead them into a succession of careers.

Lively and articulate, ENFPs inspire with their vision of new horizons. They are at the forefront as energetic advocates of change, championing causes and rallying support, and as group catalysts who draw out others and foster co-operation. The dramatic flair that puts ENFPs at centre-stage is undergirded by a wise, perceptive insight into people, enhancing their skills in interpersonal dynamics. They enjoy attracting others through their bright optimism, warmth and innate charm.

ENFPs exude enthusiasm, yet beneath their spontaneous, sometimes chaotic exterior lies a loyalty to consistent values that uphold an individual's worth and right to self-expression, and the primacy of human considerations over institutional demands.

ENFPs give life their full emotional investment, and delight in all its exciting opportunities for discovery. They confidently follow their inspirations into many a risky venture. Highly gregarious and constantly captivated by new people and fresh ideas, ENFPs find their days overflow with an abundance of things on the go. They may also express their imagination through creative or performing arts – when there's time to pursue them.

How they connect

ENFPs connect personally via their emotions, ardent to be included in whatever or whoever is the latest arena of engagement.

God for ENFPs is the source of endlessly expanding horizons and deepening harmony within and between people. Their active minds seek to discover and understand how 'in him all things hold to-gether'. ENFPs meet God in expressive worship with others, where they may sense a warm touch of his presence, and in immediate, intense prayers as the need arises. They eschew church traditions that lack personal meaning or flexibility. ENFPs' spiritual imagina-tion is fired by an inclusive range of stimuli: personal testimony, the arts or Creation.

Connecting with others is intrinsic to ENFPs' way of being. Their sociability and genuine interest in understanding and accepting others helps them relate easily to all types. Reluctant to categorize others and resistant to being defined and confined themselves, ENFPs' egalitarian outlook and empathy brings them alongside people at their own level to identify with their hopes and fears. Their sensitivity to what will please, and facility in adapting their behaviour to suit, assures them of a warm reception in many settings. For ENFPs, life is a party – or can be turned into one, as their charisma, joyful exuberance and sense of humour introduce a feel-good factor to any gathering.

ENFPs' approach to others is as intense as it is playful. They strive for authenticity, and may have some treasured soul-mates amid their extensive social circle. Idealistic ENFPs continually quest for perfection in connection. They devotedly nurture their personal relationships, keeping romance alive through fresh experiences and generous expressions of affection, both verbal and physical. ENFPs are eager both to affirm others and receive affirmation in return. Though considerately intended, ENFPs' push for relational growth may be experienced as overwhelming at times. As they live at their emotional edge, ENFPs feel criticism or conflict very personally.

ENFPs' aspirations to personal integrity mean they seek to stay connected with *themselves*, monitoring their feelings and motives. However, as the thrill of new people, ideas and projects fires their energy, ENFPs' inner links may weaken, with space for relaxation and reflection filled with activity.

While their home *environment* is more as a base for exploration than an attractive, ordered space, ENFPs are attuned to the natural world's beauty and grandeur. Quick to grasp a global perspective, ENFPs' concern for the future welfare of planet and people may result in their throwing themselves heart and soul into creative en-vironmental projects and fervently marshalling others' support.

ENTP

Keywords

Creative	Challenging
Independent	Enterprising
Analytical	Theoretical
Adaptable	Resourceful
Lively-minded	Captivating

At their best

ENTPs' energy sparkles outwardly in a glittering firework display of possibilities, patterns and potential. They scan the horizon, intuitively absorbing ideas and images, and analysing their rich harvest of impressions rationally to envision new approaches and creative strategies. Engagingly persuasive and lively-minded, ENTPs motivate others towards a brighter destiny. They are advocates of change, able both to grasp immediately and to understand deeply the fundamentals of all they survey. Though highly versatile, ENTPs flourish best with free rein to use their gifts of ingenuity and insight to originate projects and solve a succession of complex problems.

ENTPs' progressive thinking overflows in interaction as they explore and develop their ideas. They are clever and stimulating conversationalists, eager to debate issues, challenge assumptions and acquire knowledge. As the enthusiasm of these confident entrepreneurs captivates others, they raise aspirations and gain support for their schemes. But despite the effectiveness of their communication and social skills, ENTPs' mindset is essentially project-oriented, with a theoretical emphasis.

ENTPs may appear careless at those times when they lose momentum in an undertaking or relationship, but it is more likely that passion for the latest project has overtaken them. The challenge of a new frontier is their lifeblood; ENTPs are consistent in their commitment to exploring untried avenues.

ENTPs sit light to the procedures or traditions of a system. As optimistic visionaries, they are always seeking an improved model to break the old mould and may playfully challenge the status quo. They are independent, spontaneous opportunists who desire maximum flexibility to imagine possibilities rather than implement plans.

How they connect

ENTPs thrive on the stimulation connections bring them, as their mental energy seizes upon all the possibilities and challenges they see coming their way.

For ENTPs, *God* is the Creator of a dynamic cosmos that expresses his limitless complexity. He continues to act spontaneously within it, uncontained by religious traditions or human definition. ENTPs are excited by the vision of sharing in the Almighty's activity in his universe. They meet God as they participate in contemporary worship, conversational prayer or cutting-edge theological dialogue about forging creative ways to cut through the constraints of church past and be open to the coming Kingdom.

Outgoing and good-humoured, ENTPs can connect with most types of *people*. They especially enjoy the company of like-minded enthusiasts for ideas, who offer opportunities for ENTPs' love of learning through intellectual interaction. Their passion for betterment carries over into their personal relationships, which become valued arenas of growth and mutual development. ENTPs' concern for a relationship's direction motivates their active investment in it, though they also like to preserve a certain amount of independence. Their passion for possibilities can work two ways: ENTPs may discern the potential for another's personal growth – a worthy project in itself – or focus on how the other might contribute to whatever scheme the ENTP currently has up and running.

ENTPs possess considerable acumen concerning others' motives and attitudes. They typically seek to understand rather than judge, but may not easily sympathize with those who experience life differently. The love of debate that leads them to adopt contrary positions for the sheer fun of arguing an alternative point of view is best engaged in with a partner who can hold their own. At times ENTPs' playful challenges may harbour a competitive edge: they are not above practising one-upmanship even within their friendship circle, but also need others' appreciation to nurture their own self-esteem. ENTPs may not realize how others may experience their tireless energy: inspiring, but at times also tiring.

The allure of outer exploration may leave ENTPs scant space or inclination for inner reflection or *self-awareness*. They may even 'forget' their physical needs in the heat of activity. Using their analytical skills inwardly also challenges ENTPs to choose priorities and values that could limit their room for manoeuvre.

ENTPs may be full of ingenious strategies to save the planet, based on a knowledgeable understanding of the intricacies of both God-generated and man-made systems. They may focus more on projects concerning the *environment*'s future than on enjoying Creation now. Acts of responsible stewardship, e.g. recycling, may lose their lustre as they become routine.

ESTJ

Keywords

Organized	Direct
Decisive	Realistic
Efficient	Logical
Structured	Diligent
Dependable	Dispassionate

At their best

ESTJs' energy gushes outwards like a powerful avalanche, forcefully rearranging all in its path. Drawing on factual information acquired via their senses, ESTJs take charge to get things done. They thrive at assessing situations, making plans, mobilizing resources and directing operations efficiently to meet required objectives. Their practical service is seen at its best in designated administrative roles within organizations, where ESTJs have authority to manage systems and supervise procedures according to accepted guidelines.

Logical and decisive, ESTJs quickly come to an understanding of how things ought to run, based on their expertise and experience. They respect the established order and seek to uphold it, both as rule-makers and as rule-followers. Their methodical approach to solving problems and implementing plans is characterized by dutiful discipline, undeterred by practical obstacles or personal cost. ESTJs put great energy into their work and may be regarded as pillars of their communities. They enjoy seeing tangible results and rewards for their labours, preferably immediately.

Despite their task-oriented outlook, ESTJs enjoy interacting with others. Their quick wit and appetite for fun can make them socially engaging. Belonging matters: ESTJs participate loyally in family traditions and celebrations, valuing the significance of such occasions.

ESTJs' focus on clear goals is accompanied by directness in expressing their opinions and expectations. But while their forthright insistence that others should toe the line may at times seem overstrict, ESTJs are consistent in applying their exacting standards to themselves. Their principled honesty may lead them to change their own behaviour or revise their rules in the light of newly apprehended truth.

How they connect

ESTJs connect via their commitment to the collective, and their desire to contribute to a system beyond themselves.

God for ESTJs is primarily judge and guardian. He expresses order through Creation, which runs according to his plan. He is faithful, and grounded in existence since before time began. ESTJs' have awe for God's authority over the cosmos and their humble place within it. They meet him in the routine of structured worship with others, and serve him through practical action. ESTJs faithfully uphold the Church and its traditions as embodying the divine order in day-by-day community living.

ESTJs *connect with others* corporately in organized groupings of family, church or work. Their straightforward, friendly self-confidence makes them easy to get to know, and their willingness to take responsibility may draw them into leadership roles. ESTJs play a valuable part in maintaining group stability; adhering to the principles of established structures transcends considerations of individual finer feelings. This may sometimes result in ESTJs' personal lack of tact in dealing with those they sense are violating those principles. At their best, ESTJs can be relied upon to act fairly, and serve people by working on their behalf to keep the wider group viable and secure.

Although ESTJs are more drawn to the wider social horizon than intimate one-to-one interactions, they value integrity in their personal relationships, taking their roles seriously and making faithful, lifelong ties. ESTJs regard their ongoing loyalty as saying all that is needed regarding their emotional commitment: they are generally more comfortable with receiving respect and gratitude than affection, but do need recognition for their accomplishments. ESTJs like to know where they stand in a relationship. They connect most easily in defined roles, and in using their knowledge to help another. If conflict arises, they are ready to face and resolve it.

ESTJs relate to *themselves* via their functional roles. Their identity is strongly linked to a sense of their own capabilities. If their contribution is no longer needed, ESTJs' self-worth may suffer loss. ESTJs may dismiss their 'illogical' inner emotional life, ignoring hurt feelings and trying to carry on as normal for as long as they are able.

ESTJs are very consciously connected to their immediate *environment*, organizing their surroundings so that all is tidy and in its allotted place. They may struggle to imagine future theoretical environmental scenarios, but will happily supervise the smooth running of projects with specific practical goals, ensuring any decisions about good practice are consistently followed through by all.

ESFJ

Keywords

Warm	Caring
Co-operative	Responsible
Sociable	Organized
Loyal	Traditional
Hospitable	Tactful

At their best

ESFJs' energy radiates outwards, encompassing others in sun-like rays of warmth. Using their senses to 'read' people, ESFJs pick up a wide range of accurate, personal information. They delight in directing what they detect into precisely planned and efficiently executed actions to meet others' needs and desires. ESFJs naturally take care and take charge. They flourish in clear roles where they can use their personable manner to bring harmony, and organize situations to serve everyone's well-being, often in public-service occupations.

ESFJs are found wherever people are gathered: in organizations, families and churches. Their clearly defined values and awareness of appropriate behaviour make them at home within established community frameworks. As loyal, active members, ESFJs nurture fellowship by drawing others into shared activities. Their concern to please is matched by a respect for those in authority. ESFJs prize stability and faithfully uphold institutions. They prefer to meet expectations and observe traditions rather than rock the boat.

ESFJs' industry on others' behalf may result in them handling multiple roles with apparent ease. Others may not realize the extent of their efforts, or see that underneath their capable, generous exterior, ESFJs really need to be appreciated for what they give and who they are. Highly sociable and hospitable, ESFJs enjoy talking and finding things out. They think best in conversation and are gifted networkers: informed and informative, emotionally expressive and articulate about their views. Compassion motivates them to be effective listeners who remember significant personal detail and ensure others feel cared for in thoughtful acts of kindness, perhaps by marking a special occasion with a personal touch.

How they connect

For ESFJs, connection opens up channels of vitality enabling warmth, personal meaning, direction and a sense of identity to flow into their lives.

God for ESFJs is the compassionate Father, who has made and sustains the created order. They respond in personal trust as his children, offering their love, obeying his commandments and cherishing his Creation. ESFJs' worship may be structured and involve the senses through music or sacrament. It will certainly be expressive, as they pour out spoken prayers and sung praises in love for God and joy in their personal friendship with him. ESFJs may also value prayer shared with others, as it embodies the unity they seek above all.

ESFJs' yearning for harmonious human contact impels them towards *connection with others*. Their responsiveness to others' behaviour, appearance and feelings, and their tactful manner, enables ESFJs to create a rapport with many. Hospitable, warm-hearted and gracious, ESFJs use every opportunity to bring people together and make them feel good, often through social occasions. Co-operation is paramount: ESFJs may adapt to the prevailing social climate of their environment to achieve it. They set a high premium on personal loyalty and maintaining stable relationships, often expressing care through practical service. ESFJs support those they love, and seek to bring out the best in them that sometimes only they can see.

ESFJs connect with others to discover their own values, as they look to authoritative sources to help clarify their own opinions and attitudes. Once these are formulated, ESFJs are extremely clear and vocal about what they expect from themselves – and others. Ever sensitive to others' responses, ESFJs long to be affirmed. Lack of positive feedback can leave them bruised by indifference and feeling like mere functionaries. Their desire for warm relationships may mean they struggle to acknowledge the negative aspects of those special to them. They may deny conflicts rather than experience the discomfort of dealing with them.

ESFJs connect with *themselves* primarily through their social roles. Their orientation to action may leave little space for reflection, and they can risk losing touch with who they essentially are. They may also avoid looking inwards if it entails facing 'unacceptable' and guilt-inducing negative feelings.

ESFJs savour their *surroundings* through all their senses. They care for their possessions and keep their homes neat, attractive and welcoming. ESFJs also appreciate beauty and harmony in the natural world. Safeguarding tomorrow's environment is seen in terms of today's stewardship. Promoting practical action or organizing a group project may be particularly meaningful for them.

ENFJ

Keywords

Articulate	Warm
Empathetic	Caring
Inspiring	Loyal
Encouraging	Enthusiastic
Idealistic	Diplomatic

At their best

ENFJs' energy radiates outward like the inviting warmth of a camp-fire. Focusing their attention on people, ENFJs use empathic sensitivity to deepen their understanding, gain insight and envision possibilities. They channel what they discern into a passionate enthusiasm for releasing individual potential and creating inter-personal harmony. ENFJs excel wherever they can serve humanity by working co-operatively for others' well-being and development in a harmonious and structured setting, possibly in education, psychology, church life or personnel work.

ENFJs are decisive, confident facilitators of groups and enablers of individuals. They are eager to engage others personally, listening and responding with warm concern and natural tact. Their charisma, approachability and accomplished social skills generally ensure they gravitate towards a leadership role. ENFJs evince an instinctive sense of a group's dynamics, clear vision for its direction and a deft touch in building consensus. Optimistic and determined to bring out the best in others, ENFJs make inspiring and popular leaders.

In their zeal for offering care and support, ENFJs may easily hide their own emotional needs as they absorb others' feelings. Yet beneath their confident exterior lies a tender sensitivity to criticism that craves the soothing balm of a warm, appreciative response.

ENFJs' interactions are enhanced by their gifts of communication. Always open to new possibilities, they structure and express their ideas clearly. They have an easy facility with words, which they prefer to exercise face-to-face rather than on paper. ENFJs are articulate, persuasive and entertaining speakers who may powerfully influence others for good, perhaps by leading them into life-changing decisions.

How they connect

ENFJs connect through the heart, at their best and most fully themselves when invigorated and stimulated by contact with others.

God for ENFJs is the Creator of a delightful and diverse humanity, the source of glorious possibilities for wholeness and harmony, as he reaches out personally to welcome his people warmly in all-embracing grace. ENFJs see God in the faces of those made in his image. They meet him in prayer of all kinds, but particularly expressive, relaxed and spontaneous prayer with others, as they come to their Maker, fully assured of his acceptance, to sense his powerful, healing presence. Shared silence may appeal more than solitary contemplation.

ENFJs' lifeblood is in meaningful *interpersonal connections*. Congenial, compassionate and gracious, they engage easily with many, and are likely to have a wide friendship circle. They flourish in company, radiating warmth, as they reach out to feel for the hearts of those around them. They strive to ensure that personal or social occasions are happy, affirming and memorable. One-to-one, ENFJs are committed to pursuing authentic, lifelong relationships, and others may look to them for understanding, support and nurture. They are considerate, loving and generous in expressing affection in word and deed. The high value they place on personal relationships is reflected in their loyalty, honesty and attentiveness. For even-tempered ENFJs, love will always have the last word, whatever the rules dictate.

ENFJs' desire for harmony and good feeling colours their personal connections. They may refrain from expressing strong opinions, give way in an argument, or accede to others' emotional demands rather than flag up their own needs – despite feeling hurt when ignored. Yet ENFJs may bring an active intensity to developing their personal relationships according to their own clear vision of the way things should be. As idealists, they focus on what is admirable in others and aim for excellence in their relationships.

ENFJs connect with *themselves* via caring involvement with others, from which they gain much personal fulfilment. Their positive self-image may be threatened by inner negative feelings. Thus ENFJs may avoid too much introspective time alone. They may also interpret personal need as a sign of weakness.

ENFJs prefer structure and order around them. They may not always be aware of the finer details of their physical *surroundings*, but their attunement to people sensitizes them to atmosphere, which they long to be harmonious. Concern for environmental issues will resonate with them wherever it is linked to concerns for humanity, particularly its future welfare.

ENTJ

Keywords

Decisive	Lively-minded
Innovative	Directive

Theoretical   Principled
Strategic   Articulate
Challenging   Undaunted

At their best

ENTJs' energy propels outwards like a whirlwind sweeping up all within its range. Their able minds quickly grasp an understanding of the situations and structures they survey, and their intuition gives them an eye for ways to shape and improve them. Their organizational abilities, professionalism and decisiveness in taking initiatives make ENTJs natural leaders in whatever field they enter.

ENTJs stride across the landscape in resolute pursuit of integrity and excellence. Their gift of analytical thinking is supported by an appetite for the knowledge they need to be stimulated and inspired. They turn their minds to developing strategies to make their vision a reality within their own sphere of influence. They are articulate and direct communicators, and confidently marshal all available resources towards achieving their goals.

ENTJs may appear uncaring in their visionary drive, overpowering energy and dedication to correcting flaws and failings. They are, however, far from unfeeling. Their approach may be rational and objective, but their deep passion is seen in the disciplined, personal investment they make in pursuit of their call. It is not easy to get ENTJs off the job, so committed are they to implementing their dream of a better world.

As lovers of the truth, ENTJs are willing to put themselves under the searing spotlight of their own critique. Yet ultimately their focus on the distant horizon, uncluttered by inconsequential details and finer feelings, means they can accomplish great things for God, often taking his people beyond where they would have the courage and vision to venture themselves.

How they connect

ENTJs connect through the mind and by taking the lead in whatever shared enterprise they find themselves.

God for ENTJs is the omnipotent and active architect of the universe. They strive to understand the character and workings of this awesome being rationally through the study of his word and his world. ENTJs are fearless in pursuing the truth, however discomforting its implications. Their dedication may be seen in a disciplined devotional life, alongside tenacity in wrestling with theological complexities, which means far more than the impersonal acquisition of head-knowledge: a breakthrough to new insight can lead to real excitement and spiritual growth, especially as ENTJs find ways of applying what they have learned, to bring about creative change towards greater godliness.

ENTJs' approach to *relationships* is characterized by active commitment, loyalty and fairness. They are direct rather than tender, and not naturally sensitive to the emotional nuances in others' responses. Small-talk and conversation to establish rapport and intimacy are not their métier: they prefer engaging in intellectual debate, problem-solving or exchanging knowledge. Their energy for excellence may sometimes come across as critical or impatient of others, but they may be surprised to discover they have been felt as harsh or unsupportive.

As forthright personalities, ENTJs welcome and respect those who will respond to them with similar directness. Given their confident presentation, this may not happen to ENTJs too often. However, those who rise to the challenge are likely to find ENTJs willing to hear a well-argued alternative viewpoint and shift their position if convinced of the merits of doing so.

ENTJs connect with *themselves* in a clear-thinking honesty that may emerge in a rigorous approach to establishing an efficient lifestyle based on principles of objective truth. They may make logical plans for themselves to regulate their behaviour. ENTJs may value individual time to think things through, but are not inclined to spend long fine-tuning personal development or exploring inner feelings, when the outer world needs organizing.

ENTJs' response to the wider *environment* may comprise intellectual curiosity and a sense of wonder at the complexity of the created order. They may be keenly aware of their God-given responsibility to exercise intelligent and just stewardship. Their long-range vision enables them to engage with the call to decisive action now to preserve the planet for future generations. This can fuel their energy in campaigning for individual and wider structural change.

4

A step further

-------•◦•-------

A firm grounding

Time and again on a Myers-Briggs® workshop, people are delighted when they find their 'best-fit type'. There are comments such as 'That's just me', or 'When I read that description, I recognized myself right away'. Perhaps this was your experience in reading your reported type among the 16 presented in the last chapter. It can be a relief to find that what we may have assumed to be our own quirkiness, or just a disconnected random set of attributes, actually coheres into a distinct personality shape.

A key message of the Myers-Briggs Type Indicator® model is 'It's OK to be me', with no one personality type singled out as superior to any other. Indeed, Isabel Myers' own book, *Gifts Differing*, takes its title from Romans 12.6, acknowledging that, 'we have gifts that differ . . .' Created in God's image, we can live with permission to cherish our God-given personality, rather than under compulsion to strive to be someone else.

As John, who reported as Introvert, commented, 'I used to think being introverted was inferior. Now I realize it's just different.' In a society oriented towards the outer world of appearance, activity and engagement, it was liberating to realize the value of the more selective, inward focus of an Introvert preference.

For Helen, recognizing her Thinking preference became a 'penny-dropping' moment. Now a young adult, she was struck by expectations on her as she grew up in a Feeling family. She'd always assumed there was something wrong with her when she was told she was cold and unfeeling. Identifying her true preference helped Helen appreciate her strengths of objective judgement and analysis, and made a positive impact on family relationships when they talked over this discovery together.

Clarifying our 'best-fit type' not only helps us see our personality's pattern, it also underlines our particular gifts, so we can recognize more clearly what we distinctively offer the wider group. What one person may assume is ordinary and unremarkable – such as a J penchant for planning and organizing – may look quite different through the eyes of another type. An ISFJ who felt he was nothing special was astonished to hear a free-wheeling ESFP at the same workshop speak of her admiration for those who could follow through on their commitments and actually meet deadlines.

Knowing who we are can also improve relationships. One married couple, Liz (J preference) and Rob (P preference), found it helped their communication. Every Saturday morning, when Rob asked Liz, 'What are we doing today?' J Liz panicked, thinking she ought to come up with a schedule. But P Rob's question did not mean, 'What have you planned?' but 'What are the possibilities for what we *might* do?' Realizing the assumptions they made from their different personality perspectives helped ease Liz and Rob into their weekends.

Since operating in line with our natural preferences comes more easily to us than going against the grain on our less-preferred side, simply identifying our personality type can enable us to maintain greater well-being. This was so for Tania.

Tania had marked herself down as an Extravert, but it was the Introvert counterpart to her reported Myers-Briggs profile that most deeply resonated with her. Tania's upbringing had trained her in developing effective extraverting skills, but becoming aware of her I preference helped Tania see why she could find life so draining. She began to build in more time for quietness, and started exploring contemplative prayer, soon experiencing the benefits in her life in church, at work and at home.

So before we seek any further insights for spiritual direction, it is worth taking note of how simply knowing ourselves and our acceptability can have a profound impact in itself, bringing new freedom and holding implications for development. Knowing our Myers-Briggs personality type profile can help us:

1 gain a more settled grounding in our own valuable God-given gifts of personality;
2 acknowledge there can be various and equally valid ways of relating to God;

3 value and appreciate gifts that others have;

4 understand why some of our relationships may need more working at than others;

5 increase our patience with others as we see they are being different rather than difficult;

6 realize areas where we may need the support or insight of another's perspective;

7 allow ourselves to be ourselves and others to be themselves;

8 value and appreciate gifts we may not have realized we have;

9 become alert to blind spots of which we were previously unaware;

10 identify what drains and resources us, so we can balance our living more effectively.

For reflection

Read Psalm 139.1–6, reflecting on the Lord's total knowledge of you. Then read v. 23 as a personal prayer.

Re-read your MBTI 'best-fit' profile in the light of the ten points listed above. What thoughts or feelings does this prompt about your own outlook, situation or relationships? Where might these insights take you?

Record your reflections in a journal or, if you prefer, talk them through with a trusted friend.

Our place on the Myers-Briggs chart can be the start of a new stage in our Christian journey. The first essential in any journey is to know where we're setting out from; the second is to be clear where we're heading to. In type terms, these are ultimately one and the same. Grounded in the knowledge of our basic personality types, our destination is the redeemed, sanctified and matured expression of our personality in Christ. We are not being conformed and confined into one of 16 personality type moulds. The infinite variety that emerges from our different preference strengths, experiences, backgrounds, life-choices, habits and tastes results in an endless range of unique individuals, with certain identifiable and distinctive brush-strokes of the Creator in common.

The ultimate aim of any spiritual direction is to strengthen connection: where humankind was split apart through breaking the
fundamental connection of loving trust in the Creator, Jesus has
opened up the Way of redemption, reconnection and re-creation.
Just as our faith journey involves growing in loving connection with
God, others, our environment and ourselves, so it involves nurturing healthy inward connections. These come to fruition as we move
towards being integrated personalities, reconciled and at peace in
ourselves. At this point, it's worth noting that the personality
profiles in the last chapter presented the types 'at their best', and
for many of us there's more than a little way to go to get there!

To know how the Myers-Briggs model can give us insights to
help us on our way, we need to look further into how the different personality elements interconnect, so our type profile is not
merely a description but suggests some direction.

More than four letters

Whether you looked at several profiles before seeing yourself
reflected, or simply enjoyed reading through them for your own
interest, it will be clear your particular collection of Myers-Briggs
letters is more than four separate beads strung in a line.

The profiles created when preferences are combined gain their
distinctiveness from how these preferences interact. The impact of
one on another has implications for the focus and emphasis, gifts
and blind spots, flows and tensions in our complete personality. For
example, consider our **function** letters (see Figure 3).

Perceiving function N takes in information across a broad spectrum, with a vision for possibilities and patterns, but while

N + *Judging* T = NT focus on creative possibilities in *impersonal
structures*
N + *Judging* F = NF focus on creative possibilities for *people.*

Attitude	Functions		Attitude
	Perceiving	*Judging*	
Extravert	Sensing	Thinking	Judging
Introvert	iNtuition	Feeling	Perceiving

Figure 3 The Myers-Briggs letters

Perceiving function S takes in information in a detailed way, with an eye for facts, and measurable and material realities, but while

S + *Judging* T = ST focus on practicalities in maintaining *systems*
S + *Judging* F = SF focus on practicalities in caring for *people's* current needs.

From flat-pack to 3-D landscape

Apart from the interaction between our reported preference letters, our *less-preferred* letters play a vital part in the wholeness of our individual personalities: our Myers-Briggs profile has a vertical as well as a horizontal dimension.

One of the reactions people express when learning about Myers-Briggs preferences and being asked to choose between two alternatives is, 'But I do both!' They are right, of course. We all use *both* aspects of every preference, according to our needs, circumstances or requirements of our situation. Although we will experience one preference in each pair as more natural to us, with enough practice, we may also develop considerable skills in our less-preferred arenas. Drawing on our less-preferred side is not just an unfortunate necessity; it is vital to our effective functioning in life and the balance of our personalities. For example, consider the **attitude** letters:

Those with an E preference for the energy and action of the outer world need the balance of some 'I time' in reflection to take stock and understand what is going on within, if they are not to spend life in shallow activity, disconnected from their inner selves.

Those with an I preference for the resourcing and reflection of the inner world need the balance of some 'E time' in action to engage, and bring to light and fruition what is within, if they are not to spend life in deep stagnation, disconnected from the outer world. (For many Is, however, the pressure can be all the other way: the outer world's constant demands for attention make it hard to preserve the private space they need to regain their energies.)

Those with a J preference for the order, discipline and closure it brings need the balance of some 'P time' for spontaneity, if they are not to become rigid, controlling and overly brittle when their best-laid plans meet obstacles and need adapting or adjusting.

Those with a **P** preference for the opportunity, freedom and open-endedness it brings need the balance of some 'J time' for decisiveness, if they are not to become indulgent, wayward and reluctant to commit to and follow through plans to completion and fruition.

Light and shadow

The four letters of our Myers-Briggs profile represent what is above the surface and in the light. This is the person we are conscious of being. Yet our less-preferred side also lives within us, albeit in the shadow. So if we are looking at the two types **INTJ** and **ESFP**, for example, what is in the light in one profile forms the other type's shadow side.

	I	N	T	J
Shadow	E	S	F	P

but,

	E	S	F	P
Shadow	I	N	T	J

No wonder different personalities may struggle to understand one another! One person's preference can be precisely the area another avoids wherever possible. Yet the less-preferred side lying in our personality's shadow-lands needs to be allowed some expression and not just remain dormant as our unlived life. The particular balance-point between different preferences will vary according to our type: an **INTJ** will have a greater weighting towards expressing an Introvert preference than an **ESFP**. But both need both.

If we refuse to engage with our less-preferred side, we ultimately become caricatures of ourselves, rather than whole people. If we *are* willing to engage with our shadow side, it can be a great area of challenge and creativity: a psychologically and spiritually strategic place of growth. Finding our spiritual direction will at some point involve mustering the faith to move beyond our comfort zone and explore less familiar territory, where we feel more vulnerable and less in control. It will mean trusting God as Lord of every part of us, including aspects of ourselves we can be tempted to reject or neglect.

A biblical illustration of this could be seen in Peter's vision at Joppa and ensuing events (Acts 10), where it becomes clear that God's purposes in Christ go beyond the Jews to include the Gentiles. Peter sees a vision of animals that Jewish law declares unclean, and is astonished to hear the divine command to 'Kill and eat.' Significantly, he receives this communication when in a trance. In an unconscious state, our lowered defences may make us more receptive to unprecedented possibilities than when we are awake and alert.

As the vision's message is confirmed by the visit of Gentile Cornelius, who testifies to God's call to him and upon whose household the Holy Spirit falls as powerfully as on Jewish Christian converts, Peter sees God is at work. He acknowledges God is breaking through old structures and expectations to affirm his mercy on the Gentiles. The less-preferred people come out of the shadows into Christ's light, to be included in God's Kingdom, which is incomplete without them. They joined those who had been used to living as the God-preferred people, an inclusion the early Church initially found awkwardly unexpected.

Finding our spiritual direction will involve welcoming in some 'Gentile' aspects of our personalities. What we may have tended to exclude as unacceptable has a place in the wholeness of our complete personalities.

Introducing dynamics

So far we have seen that our personality preferences are not four aspects operating independently, but interconnect and impact on one another. We have noted how we all use each preference at times, and observed that this is needed for our effectiveness and for growth to maturity. We have seen that optimum development is not to use the different preferences equally, but to come to a balance between them that reflects our particular personality profile. Finally, we have noted that engaging with our less-preferred or shadow side can be challenging but enriching. It is now time to explore in more detail how our personality preferences interrelate.

It will help to remind ourselves how the Myers-Briggs personality preferences are grouped: see Figure 4.

To start exploring our type's dynamics, we need to focus on the middle function letters. We all use all four functions to some degree.

Attitude	Functions		Attitude
	Perceiving	*Judging*	
E	S	T	J
or	or	or	or
I	N	F	P
Source of energy	Gathering information	Making decisions	Our lifestyle

Figure 4 How the personality preferences are grouped

However, our particular personality shapes the order and extent of that use. In other words, the functions operate within us in a hierarchy: 1, 2, 3, 4, or in Myers-Briggs terms: **Dominant, Auxiliary, Tertiary** and **Inferior**. If we imagine our life as a stage play, our **Dominant** function plays the lead role, while the other functions are like members of the supporting cast. The **Inferior** may scarcely be seen on stage, but, as with many plays, the 'bit part' can make a dramatic and strategic contribution to plot and performance.

We also use each function in a particular *orientation*, either,

directed *outwards* to the world of actions and words in an *extra-verted* way, or
directed *inwards* to the world of thoughts and feelings, in an *intro-verted* way.

The functions in descending order

1 Dominant

Our **Dominant** function forms our personality's linchpin. It is our best-developed process, the one we rely on most. It takes the lead role, defining our core characteristics and unifying our personality.

Our **Dominant** is our *favourite function*,
    either a *Perceiving* function – S or N
    or a *Judging* function – T or F.
It is used in our *favourite world* (outer or inner) – E or I.

2 Auxiliary

Our **Auxiliary** function plays a vital role in supporting and *complementing* our **Dominant** function. It is the *other* letter of our personality type's *function* pair. So,

Either **Dominant** = *Perceiving* function (S or N)
(Gathers information) and
Auxiliary = *Judging* function (T or F)
(Helps by deciding what to do with it)

Or **Dominant** = *Judging* function (T or F)
(Makes decisions) and
Auxiliary = *Perceiving* function (S or N)
(Helps by providing information).

With our **Dominant** attention directed towards our favourite world, our **Auxiliary** brings a necessary balance by functioning in the *opposite orientation*. So:

Dominant used in outer world (E) means **Auxiliary** used in inner world (I).

Dominant used in inner world (I) means **Auxiliary** used in outer world (E).

3 Tertiary

Our **Tertiary** function brings us into more shadowy areas. It is one of our less-preferred functions, and the *opposite* of our **Auxiliary**. So:

Auxiliary = *Perceiving* function S then **Tertiary** = *Perceiving* function N (and vice versa).

Auxiliary = *Judging* function T then **Tertiary** = *Judging* function F (and vice versa).

While our **Tertiary** complements our **Auxiliary** and forms a vital element in our whole personality, it remains slightly mysterious. Opinion is divided as to whether it is oriented towards our outer or inner world (E or I).

4 Inferior

Our **Inferior** function lies most deeply in our personality's shadow side; as our least-preferred function, it is the *opposite* of our

Dominant. Since our **Dominant** commands the space of our favourite world, our **Inferior** is left to function in the opposite orientation – our *less* favourite world.

Our **Inferior** is our *least favourite function*,
  either a *Perceiving* function – S or N
  or a *Judging* function – T or F.
It is used in our *less favourite world* (outer or inner) – E or I.

So,

where **Dominant** = *Perceiving* function N used in an *Extraverted* orientation (**Ne**)
then **Inferior** = *Perceiving* function S used in an *Introverted* orientation (**Si**)

and,

where **Dominant** = *Judging* function F used in an *Introverted* orientation (**Fi**)
then **Inferior** = *Judging* function T used in an *Extraverted* orientation (**Te**).

Our **Inferior** function is the one of which we are least naturally conscious, the function we have paid the least attention to developing. It can be a fruitful source of creativity, and holds much unconscious potential. However, lack of confidence in our ability to use our **Inferior** means we may continue to shy away from it. As we shall see later, such avoidance can cause us difficulties with our **Inferior** function at times when we are under stress and our conscious control of our personality is weaker.

For now, you may wish to check your understanding so far by answering the questions on page 70. Answers are at the end of the chapter.

Working it out

By now you may want to know your own personality type dynamics. To work this out, we first need to find our **Dominant** function (*our favourite function in our favourite world*).

Our profile's last letter, J or P, tells us which function we like using best in our *outer* world:

Understanding dynamics 1

1 My type is INFP. What is my 'shadow' personality type?
2 My type is ESTJ. What will be the orientation of my dominant function?
3 Is the function pairing S/N a perceiving one or a judging one?
4 My Dominant function is Extraverted Intuition. What is my Inferior function?
5 My Inferior function is Introverted Thinking. What is my Dominant function?
6 My Auxiliary function is Sensing. What is my Tertiary function?
7 My Tertiary function is Thinking. What is my Auxiliary function?

P = a preference for using a *Perceiving* function in the *outer* world: **S** or **N**

J = a preference for using a *Judging* function in the *outer* world: **T** or **F**

So:

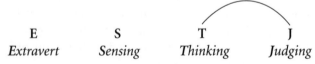

E	**S**	**T**	**J**
Extravert	*Sensing*	*Thinking*	*Judging*

J tells us **ESTJs** prefer using their *Judging* function of Thinking in the *outer* world.

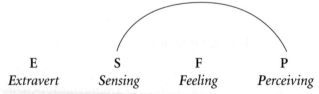

E	**S**	**F**	**P**
Extravert	*Sensing*	*Feeling*	*Perceiving*

P tells us **ESFPs** prefer using their *Perceiving* function of Sensing in the *outer* world.

We can see from their first letter, E, that **ESTJs** and **ESFPs** prefer the *outer* world. This gives us a match: we have already found their favourite *outer* world function, and we can see that this outer world is also their favourite one. So we have found their **Dominant** function.

In the above examples,

ESTJ has a **Dominant** function of **Extraverted Thinking (Te)**.
ESFP has a **Dominant** function of **Extraverted Sensing (Se)**.

Knowing the **Dominant** function enables us to work out the rest:

ESTJ

The **Dominant** is **Extraverted Thinking (Te)**   E ⎡ *Aux:* **Si** *Dom:* **Te** ⎤ J
(Favourite function in favourite world)   I ⎣ *Ter:* N *Inf:* Fi ⎦ P
The **Auxiliary** is **Introverted Sensing (Si)**
(Other preferred function in the opposite orientation)
The **Tertiary** is **iNtuition (N)**
(Opposite of the Auxiliary)
The **Inferior** is **Introverted Feeling (Fi)**
(Opposite of the Dominant: least favourite function in least favourite world)

ESFP

The **Dominant** is **Extraverted Sensing (Se)**   E ⎡ *Dom:* **Se** *Aux:* **Fi** ⎤ P
(Favourite function in favourite world)   I ⎣ *Inf:* Ni *Ter:* T ⎦ J
The **Auxiliary** is **Introverted Feeling (Fi)**
(Other preferred function in the opposite orientation)
The **Tertiary** is **Thinking (T)**
(Opposite of the Auxiliary)
The **Inferior** is **Introverted iNtuition (Ni)**
(Opposite of the Dominant: least favourite function in least favourite world)

This set of steps works for Extraverted types; one further step is needed for the Introverted. Again we find which function is used in the *outer* world, by looking at the last letter, **J** or **P**.

I	**N**	**F**	**J**
Introvert	*iNtuition*	*Feeling*	*Judging*

J tells us **INFJs** prefer using the *Judging* function of Feeling in the *outer* world.

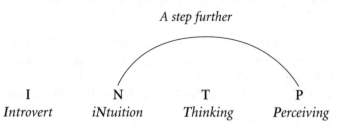

I	N	T	P
Introvert	*iNtuition*	*Thinking*	*Perceiving*

P tells us **INTPs** prefer using the *Perceiving* function of iNtuition in the *outer* world.

We can see from their first letter, **I**, that **INFJs** and **INFPs** prefer the *inner* world. We have already found their *outer* world function, but we can see that this world is the **I**'s least favourite one. This means that the other letter of their function-pair must be their **Dominant** function, as this is what they use in their favourite *inner* world.

In the above examples,

INFJ has a **Dominant** function of **Introverted iNtuition (Ni).**
INTP has a **Dominant** function of **Introverted Thinking (Ti).**

Knowing the **Dominant** function enables us to work out the rest:

INFJ

The **Dominant** is **Introverted iNtuition (Ni)**
(Favourite function in favourite world)

I ⌈**Dom: Ni Aux: Fe**⌉ J
E ⌊*Inf:*   Se *Ter:*   T⌋ P

The **Auxiliary** is **Extraverted Feeling (Fe)**
(Other preferred function in the opposite orientation)
The **Tertiary** is **Thinking (T)**
(Opposite of the Auxiliary)
The **Inferior** is **Extraverted Sensing (Se)**
(Opposite of the Dominant: least favourite function in least favourite world)

INTP

The **Dominant** is **Introverted Thinking (Ti)**
(Favourite function in favourite world)

I ⌈*Aux:* **Ne** *Dom:* **Ti**⌉ P
E ⌊*Ter:* S   *Inf:*   Fe⌋ J

The **Auxiliary** is **Extraverted iNtuition (Ne)**
(Other preferred function in the opposite orientation)
The **Tertiary** is **Sensing (S)**
(Opposite of the Auxiliary)
The **Inferior** is **Extraverted Feeling (Fe)**
(Opposite of the Dominant: least favourite function in least favourite world)

Understanding dynamics 2

As an exercise, try working through these steps with your own type or others. Check whether you are right by referring to Table 6 on page 74. Use the steps we have followed. You may wish to write your workings in a box like the one below.

1 Find the function used in the *outer* world by looking at the last letter (**P** or **J**); **P** refers to a *Perceiving* function (**S** or **N**); **J** refers to a *Judging* function (**T** or **F**).
2 Find the *favourite world* by looking at the *first letter* (**E** or **I**). You have now found the **Dominant** for **E**, but the **Auxiliary** for **I**.
3 For **I**, the **Dominant** is your other middle function letter, used in your favourite *inner* world.

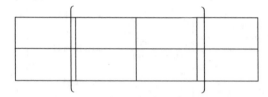

In the next chapter we will see how this deeper understanding of our personality type dynamics can suggest areas for our spiritual growth and direction. Meanwhile, here are the answers to questions posed earlier in this chapter.

Understanding dynamics 1 (Answers)

1 ESTJ
2 Extravert
3 Perceiving
4 Introverted Sensing
5 Extraverted Feeling
6 Intuition
7 Feeling

Table 6 Type dynamics

	Dominant	Auxiliary	Tertiary	Inferior
ISTJ	Introverted Sensing (**Si**)	Extraverted Thinking (**Te**)	Feeling (**F**)	Extraverted iNtuition (**Ne**)
ISFJ		Extraverted Feeling (**Fe**)	Thinking (**T**)	
INFJ	Introverted iNtuition (**Ni**)	Extraverted Feeling (**Fe**)	Thinking (**T**)	Extraverted Sensing (**Se**)
INTJ		Extraverted Thinking (**Te**)	Feeling (**F**)	
ISTP	Introverted Thinking (**Ti**)	Extraverted Sensing (**Se**)	iNtuition (**N**)	Extraverted Feeling (**Fe**)
INTP		Extraverted iNtuition (**Ne**)	Sensing (**S**)	
INFP	Introverted Feeling (**Fi**)	Extraverted iNtuition (**Ne**)	Sensing (**S**)	Extraverted Thinking (**Ti**)
ISFP		Extraverted Sensing (**Se**)	iNtuition (**N**)	
ESTP	Extraverted Sensing (**Se**)	Introverted Thinking (**Ti**)	Feeling (**F**)	Introverted iNtuition (**Ni**)
ESFP		Introverted Feeling (**Fi**)	Thinking (**T**)	
ENFP	Extraverted iNtuition (**Ne**)	Introverted Feeling (**Fi**)	Thinking (**T**)	Introverted Sensing (**Si**)
ENTP		Introverted Thinking (**Ti**)	Feeling (**F**)	
ESTJ	Extraverted Thinking (**Te**)	Introverted Sensing (**Si**)	iNtuition (**N**)	Introverted Feeling (**Fi**)
ENTJ		Introverted iNtuition (**Ni**)	Sensing (**S**)	
ENFJ	Extraverted Feeling (**Fe**)	Introverted iNtuition (**Ni**)	Sensing (**S**)	Introverted Thinking (**Ti**)
ESFJ		Introverted Sensing (**Si**)	iNtuition (**N**)	

5

Spiritual direction: paths towards wholeness

———◆•◆•◆———

Wholeness in type development

The purpose of Christian spiritual direction is to help us see where God is at already at work in our lives, and discern our next steps forward on our journey towards wholeness in Christ. Submitted to Christ's leadership, our goal is to grow up in him, with the light of his character shining through the mature, unique personalities we were created to be.

Jung, whose type theory underlies the MBTI® instrument, referred to our psychological growth as a process of 'individuation'. Its culmination is a complete personality that expresses inner harmony and balance, with all four functions (Sensing, Intuition, Thinking and Feeling) healthily integrated and playing their different roles effectively. Jung also suggested that our personality follows a natural, unfolding course of development throughout life.

A functioning personality

In our earliest years, our personality's functions are undifferentiated. Gradually, however, a front-runner among the four functions emerges, expressed in an Introverted or Extraverted way. This is our **Dominant**, which starts making a noticeable appearance in our consciousness from around the age of six. You may want to think back to your own childhood to reflect on whether there was evidence of your Dominant surfacing (I'm told one of my pastimes, as an Introverted iNtuitive child, was to go behind the lounge curtains to tell myself a story!).

During adolescence the complementary **Auxiliary** emerges to support and balance the Dominant. If our Dominant is a *Perceiving* function (S or N), Auxiliary *Judging* (T or F), helps us come to a decision. If our Dominant is a *Judging* function (T or F), Auxiliary *Perceiving* (S or N) helps us make decisions based on enough information. Like a good friend, the Auxiliary is alongside to support the Dominant without taking over.

The Dominant and Auxiliary are our two main, conscious functions, the 'dynamic duo' of our core personality. As we become more confident in using them by early adulthood, we start to bring our **Tertiary** function on board.

Finally, at mid-life, when our main personality strengths are well grounded, our **Inferior** function presents itself for greater integration into our personality. This is our most neglected and least developed function to date, and bringing it into conscious use can prove challenging and demanding on our energies.

The Inferior role

Because we tend to banish our Inferior function to our personality's unconscious, we may up to this point have only become aware of its existence when it has caused us trouble. When we become stretched, ill, tired or under great stress, for example, we are less able to manage our behaviour. At such times our Inferior function may 'slip the net' of conscious control and assume mastery. As an undeveloped function, our Inferior prompts actions that are childish and negative, and we can fall into the grip of some very uncharacteristic behaviours. Perhaps Paul is referring to this sort of experience when he confesses, 'I do not understand what I do. For what I want to do I do not do, but what I hate I do.'[1]

The best way to avoid this trap is to make friends with our Inferior function when we are on an even keel, so we can become more confident in using it, rather than letting it use us. It can help to develop our Inferior function through activities connected with play rather than work, where there is no pressure to achieve or succeed. Whatever we do, our Inferior will always remain our least-developed function, but we can integrate it into its rightful place in our personality, so it does not catch us unawares.

On the positive side, our Inferior function may also be a source of untried creative potential. It may be a rich avenue of spiritual connection: since this is where we are less confident of our own abilities, we may be more open to trusting and allowing God to take charge. After all, God can find us in the shadows as well as the light: as the Psalmist declares, 'darkness is as light to you'.[2]

A healthy balance

Pursuing wholeness of personality does not mean developing all the functions to an equal level: if you try to do everything in life, you end up doing nothing. In the same way, if you try to develop all the functions, you end up developing none of them. To be personally effective, our Dominant function needs to be fully developed as the star of the show, with the other functions bringing balance by playing their particular roles as appropriate.

As Leonore Thomson puts it, we grow by 'establishing a well-differentiated and focused personality, with boundaries clear enough to enable choice, relationship, commitment and all the human satisfactions thereof'.[3]

Finding a direction

We will go on to look at each personality's dynamics in more detail and suggest pathways towards greater wholeness. But these profiles need to be used in the context of your own personal circumstances and experience. The natural course of type development outlined above can be affected by other factors: birth order, upbringing, work role and the demands of parenting itself, to name just a few.

It is also worth noting that, for some, their overall personality profile does not exactly match how they prefer to connect with God in their devotional life, or at least, not in every season of life. There are no ultimate prescriptions about where we meet with God. It may help us to identify what preferences we *are* using; there is no hard and fast rule about what we *should* be using.

Below are listed some possible starting points for growth. These may suggest significant elements for you to focus on as you seek a fruitful spiritual direction from where you are now.

1 Past experience

You may have been brought up in a family of different personality types or in circumstances where your particular preferences were not encouraged and developed.

If nurture has pulled us out of shape, our current task may be to focus on strengthening our Dominant and Auxiliary functions to grow and affirm our core personality.

2 Present environment

You may be working in a job or in a way of life where you are called upon to exercise your less-preferred side. This may be draining you and limiting your opportunity to express your core personality.

If our God-given personality preferences are feeling the squeeze, our main priority may be to find space to express our Dominant or Auxiliary function to restore balance, and be resourced and refreshed.

3 Spiritual expectations

We may be in a worshipping community with particular expectations of the acceptable forms and expressions of Christian worship and prayer. If the spiritual culture and style feels consistently awkward to us, it may not be meeting the needs of our God-given personality to grow spiritually.

If our devotional life is leaving us hollow or not hitting the spot, our task may be to explore new ways of connecting with God to fill out the picture. We may need to discern what preferences are being used in our current worship climate, and focus on the missing preferences that bring connection for us. In this case, any of the Dominant, Auxiliary, Tertiary or Inferior functions could be involved.

4 Current circumstances

We may be in a time of loss, personal upheaval, major transition or stress. In such periods, it can feel as though our type is being turned inside out and upside down. If we are in a particular crisis, we may be struggling with our Inferior function at its most troublesome.

If we are in abnormal or distressing circumstances, our task may be to address these foremost issues, and to seek gentle ways of engaging with familiar and healthy ways of feeding our other preferences to bring us back to ourselves.

We may therefore find it helpful to focus on moving through our Tertiary and Auxiliary functions, back towards our Dominant, using whatever avenues we experience as most accessible and least draining to reground ourselves and our personalities.

5 On solid ground

It may be that times are good. We feel largely satisfied with our spiritual lives, but are looking for ways to go deeper with God.

If we know we are stable and securely grounded in our Dominant and Auxiliary functions, we may be ready for a new challenge. Our task may be to venture out more deliberately into shadow territory and explore developing our Inferior or Tertiary function.

The type profiles that follow highlight each personality's dynamics and offer some potential pathways towards wholeness. Use it alongside your basic profile back in Chapter 3 to explore your spiritual direction. Each profile follows a set format, including:

- **Something to celebrate** in affirming the fruitful expression of your Dominant function, with the particular angle supplied by your Auxiliary.
- **Something to challenge** in attending to the oft-neglected Inferior function, with its potential as a valuable, creative anchor-point – or a source of trouble.
- **Something to balance** in affirming the supporting role of your Auxiliary function, which needs to be sufficiently developed to balance your Dominant without over-shadowing it.
- **Something to draw on** in looking to the minimally visible but accessible Tertiary function, that completes the picture and complements your Auxiliary with another perspective.

As you find your profile below, be open to where you may need to focus your attention at this stage in your Christian journey. Remember, you can only develop one function at a time! The next chapter will suggest some development activities for all four functions in their Extraverted and Introverted attitudes.

Pathways to wholeness

ISTJ	I ⎡ *Dom:* Si *Aux:* Te ⎤ J
	E ⎣ *Inf:* Ne *Ter:* F ⎦ P

Well done, good and faithful servant! You have been faithful with a few things; I will put you in charge of many things.

(Matthew 25.23)

Journeying to wholeness for ISTJs is a step-by-step process that involves affirming their **Dominant Introverted Sensing** (Si) capacity to absorb and store selected factual information. It means celebrating their ability to identify organizational needs and their loyalty and steadfast service in response. ISTJs grow as they express their faith in practical ways, finding fulfilment in following the Maker's instructions. Securely grounded through a structured personal prayer format, ISTJs are also enriched by corporate worship: consciously being present to God with others helps them release their responsibilities. Solitary pursuits from a hands-on craft activity to recording spiritual progress in a journal may also be fruitful.

ISTJs' **Inferior Extraverted iNtuition** (Ne) helps them unlock their focus on the present to open up a vision of future horizons and the wider implications of their decisions. It nudges ISTJs to imagine new possibilities rather than maintain established procedures. It can help soften their dutiful mindset by introducing the spontaneity of play, and reminding them that being carefree need not mean being careless.

ISTJs may look askance at iNtuition as fanciful, but the resurrected Jesus upheld its worth as he called to his disciples from Lake Galilee's shores. Despite their knowledge and experience as fishermen, the disciples had toiled all night and caught nothing. Breakthrough came as Jesus told them to cast their nets from the *other* side of the boat, resulting in an abundant catch.[4]

Putting common sense on hold to brainstorm possibilities may foster this function for ISTJs. Learning to explore and experiment with no concrete result or deadline in mind may also help. ISTJs may also risk bringing imagination into their prayers, stretching their level of faith to pray bold prayers that reach out beyond present limitations towards future dreams, as they rest secure in God's grace.

If ISTJs succumb to stress, perhaps through an overload of obligations with long hours of toil, immature **Inferior Ne** may overtake them. ISTJs' clarity will disintegrate into confusion and impulsiveness. Enveloped in clouds of pessimism, they may imagine catastrophic future scenarios. At such times, ISTJs need respectful support to help them offload tasks and ventilate negative feelings. With space to reconnect with their reasoning and objective reality, ISTJs may regain confidence in their ability to take control.

ISTJs' **Dominant Si** is supported by **Auxiliary Extraverted Thinking (Te)**. This alerts ISTJs to outer problems and helps them develop practical strategies for organizing affairs so others benefit from their expertise. It helps them analyse and apply the information they have collected and categorized. At its optimum level, Thinking balances ISTJs' need to gather data with the call to put it to constructive use. Exploring challenging theological truths with others, and seeking how to live out principles of righteousness and justice, may nurture this function.

When **Te** is insufficiently developed, ISTJs will lose capacity in dealing with the outer world. They may become isolated, with a weakened sense of responsibility to others. Over-reliant on **Si**'s focus on personal experience and inner data, ISTJs may become fault-finding, unwilling to trust others' capabilities or opinions. With their internal system less open to adaptation in the light of others' input, ISTJs may become stuck in past approaches and obsessed with details.

Where **Auxiliary Te** overshadows **Dominant Si**, ISTJs are left with scant information for decision-making. Opportunity to replenish the store of sensory impressions that resources their choices will be curtailed in a preoccupation with organizing their outer world. Pushed from absorption to action, ISTJs may make over-hasty, logical judgements on limited facts.

At such times, ISTJs may use their **Tertiary Feeling (F)** to consider the personal impact of their actions. This can enhance their relationships, encouraging patience and sensitivity towards others and grace towards themselves. The Feeling function can modify ISTJs' tendency to underestimate the emotional aspect of people's needs, and prompt them to put appreciation and praise into words. Taking time to listen for feelings – their own and others' – may foster this function. ISTJs could also risk expressing emotions more openly in prayer, so that tough minds are balanced by tender hearts.

ISFJ	I ⎧ ***Dom:*** Si *Aux:* Fe ⎫ J
	E ⎩ *Inf:* Ne *Ter:* T ⎭ P

No one has greater love than this, to lay down one's life for one's friends.
(John 15.13, NRSV)

Moving towards wholeness for ISFJs involves affirming their accurate perception of others' needs through their **Dominant Introverted Sensing**'s **(Si)** focused observation on the details of people's presentation. It means cherishing their ability to respond in richly blessing others in personal and practical ways. ISFJs' **Si** is nurtured by unhurried time to select and savour their particular impressions, so each can be allocated its interior place. This strengthens ISFJs' inner template of accumulated experience that informs their approach to whatever they encounter. Regular structured prayer at set times, simple ritual actions and engaging with Creation through the senses may all be helpful.

When ISFJs become too focused on details or locked in the comfort zones of well-worn ways, their **Inferior Extraverted iNtuition** **(Ne)** can help them lift their eyes from the trees for a glimpse of the wood. iNtuition can point to new horizons and untried possibilities. Though this may raise anxieties, it may be a real growthpoint for ISFJs. They may also need iNtuition's encouragement to pause and play, as a healthy interruption to their push to complete all they feel they need to do for others.

ISFJs may be suspicious of change and the unknown, but Jesus himself declared that new wine needs to be poured into new wineskins as he spoke to his disciples in the figurative, intuitive language of a parable. Jesus underlined that his newness could not be contained in old forms.[5] He was perhaps also intuitively heralding the connection between himself and the new wine he would later make so powerfully to the disciples at the Last Supper.

Daring to dream dreams, interceding for what comes to mind rather than what is on a list, and approaching prayer as playful exploration not just dutiful execution, may all foster an intuitive element in ISFJs' spirituality. Deepening their personal trust in the faithfulness of Jesus who *is* the Way may also enable them to follow into unfamiliar, open-ended territory.

When exhausted through pressures of over-work or feeling under-appreciated, ISFJs may find unreliable **Inferior Ne** taking over. Losing their grasp of details, they may behave impulsively without their usual clear rhyme and reason for considered action. They may also feel overtaken by catastrophic convictions of future gloom and doom. At such times, ISFJs need encouragement to express their fears and receive a gentle and respectful hearing. Reconnecting with those who care for them may help ISFJs regain their equilibrium and enable them to step back and be more selective about the commitments they take on.

ISFJs' **Dominant Si** is supported by **Auxiliary Extraverted Feeling** (**Fe**), helping them direct their factual perception of others' needs into realistic, relevant and orderly service. This is a highly meaningful connection for ISFJs, who value belonging and co-operation. They may emanate quiet warmth as they make their unassuming but constructive contribution to the welfare of those around them, and take pains to express their appreciation of others. Praying with and for others in ways that articulate their feelings may help ISFJs develop this function, as well as working alongside others on joint pastoral projects.

Where **Fe** is underdeveloped, ISFJs' Sensing is left without the capacity to translate memories and impressions into a fruitful way of interacting with the world. Reserved by nature, ISFJs tend to withhold personal feelings rather than express them. But their reluctance to be assertive may not be healthy for either themselves or others.

Where **Auxiliary Fe** overshadows **Dominant Si**, ISFJs fall prey to an excessive drive to serve, and their painstaking approach becomes run ragged by trying to fulfil all their commitments. The pleasure of Sensing is crushed under outside pressures. In this state, ISFJs may avoid attending to or speaking out about their own needs in order to keep the peace, but this just means internal conflict as they become resentful. They may develop symptoms of bodily distress in order to allow themselves to rest.

Where caught up in destructive work or relationship patterns, ISFJs need to draw on their **Tertiary Thinking** (**T**) for a more objective analysis of their situation. This may involve the challenge of facing moral complexities and grappling with principles rather than practicalities. ISFJs can become trapped in unhealthy relationships through their sense of responsibility. Thinking may help them make difficult, though loving, decisions that consider the long-term implications of what they do, not just the short-term impact on people's feelings.

INFJ	I ⎡ *Dom:* Ni *Aux:* Fe ⎤ J
	E ⎣ *Inf:* Se *Ter:* T ⎦ P

No eye has seen, nor ear heard, nor the human heart conceived, what God has prepared for those who love him.

(*1 Corinthians 2.9, NRSV*)

Moving towards wholeness for INFJs involves celebrating their **Dominant Introverted iNtuition's** (**Ni**) gifts of insight and vision. It means affirming their personal interactions in their creative communication and the empathy and encouragement they express towards those around them. Personal space and time are vital to the nourishment of INFJs' primary call to the world within, allowing them to replenish their reservoir of information for reflection.

Contemplative prayer, quiet reading, reflection, heart-to-heart encounters in prayer and conversation, and stimulation via the arts may all be helpful.

Energized by the inner world of hidden connections and complex meanings, INFJs need their **Inferior Extraverted Sensing** (**Se**) to remind them that matter matters. Sensing can be a valuable anchor to the introspective excesses or mental frenzy of unchecked intuition. It may help INFJs regain a healthy balance and awareness of their bodies, which also need their care and attention. Switching to a Sensing focus may also release new fruitfulness and creativity where over-worked intuition has led to staleness or frustration.

INFJs may be tempted to undervalue the Sensing spirituality of ordinary practical living, but when the resurrected Jesus appeared to the disciples by Lake Galilee, he connected with them not through an intangible inner experience but by cooking and sharing breakfast with them.[6]

Making time for simply encountering God's Creation *as it is* through their senses, engaging in practical tasks that are 'hands-on' rather than 'head-in', can enable INFJs to 'let go and let God'.

Physical activity can help restore INFJs to the immediate reality of the present moment – perhaps literally putting their feet back on the ground. Exploring prayer through doing, rather than reflecting, may also prove fruitful.

If INFJs are under great stress, perhaps through being over-whelmed with outer demands and details, they may become vulnerable to primitive **Inferior Se** overtaking them. They may over-indulge in sensual activities such as eating or shopping, and then berate themselves for their behaviour. They may obsess over controlling their physical environment through tidying, cleaning or organizing. INFJs in this fragile position need time alone to recharge their batteries, and acceptance, as opposed to advice, from others. Afterwards they may learn to set more realistic goals and incorporate pleasurable sensing experiences in moderation into their lives.

INFJs' **Dominant Ni** is supported by **Auxiliary Extraverted Feeling** (**Fe**), helping INFJs to formulate and mediate their insights and make them accessible to others. It enables INFJs to foster harmony and offer something personally meaningful that inspires and deeply touches those around them. At its optimum level, Feeling helps INFJs organize inner perceptions, and make personal connections to express their warmth and empathy. Praying with others, particularly in intercession, participating in social activities and being willing to share as well as listen to feelings, may all foster this function.

Where **Fe** is underdeveloped, INFJs may be left isolated in their own personal universe, unable to articulate their deep convictions or insights. Their inner open-ended and free-ranging iNtuition is left dangling with no route to fulfilment or resolution. Avoiding the potential tension of Fe's pressure towards closure and commitment will be ultimately unsatisfying.

But where **Auxiliary Fe** overrides **Dominant Ni** it can smother the private space and time INFJs need for their richest inspirations to emerge from the depths. INFJs' desire for harmony becomes an inability to say no to others' demands. This can leave them spinning with indecision about how to prioritize their commitments, resentful of others' intrusion, and with their creativity fragmented and frustrated.

At such times, INFJs may need to activate their **Tertiary Thinking** (**T**) to make clear-minded decisions about what is realistically achievable rather than idealistically aspired to. Learning to draw on a more objective analytical approach may also supplement INFJs' process of sifting and developing their ideas. Their enjoyment of using their minds may make this function more accessible. Though INFJs may find the prospect a little dry, theological study may yield fruitful insights, especially when they alight upon some personal connection.

INTJ	I ⌈ *Dom:* Ni *Aux:* Te ⌉ J
	E ⌊ *Inf:* Se *Ter:* F ⌋ P

Do not conform any longer to the pattern of this world, but be transformed by the renewing of your mind. Then you will be able to test and approve what God's will is – his good, pleasing and perfect will.
(Romans 12.2)

INTJs' journey to wholeness involves celebrating their **Dominant Introverted iNtuition**'s (**Ni**) gift of inspired and original insights as they discern potential for improvement wherever they look. It means affirming their dedication to translating their innovative vision into practical strategies that benefit all. INTJs are spiritually enriched in private, contemplative prayer that brings inner transformation from self-reflection to profound God-awareness. Their disciplined devotional life may include exploring and evaluating different prayer forms, and subjecting Scripture to intelligent theological analysis that seeks the truth irrespective of tradition.

INTJs' **Inferior Extraverted Sensing** (**Se**) can encourage them to ground theory in the reality of facts and details. It can foster a healthy balance of mental activity with bodily attention, reminding them to eat and exercise as well as solve problems. It can help them relax their pursuit of perfection to live in the present moment, and learn to play with no goal in view.

INTJs may downplay physicality, but the incarnate Jesus honoured the gift of Sensing. He healed one blind man by spitting on dry earth, making mud to rub on the man's eyes, and instructing him to wash it off in a nearby pool. Though this was not vital to Jesus' act of healing, he met the man's needs for real encounter through physical contact.[7]

Taking time to smell the flowers, or to prepare and linger over a meal, can nurture this function if INTJs can simply enjoy the experience without interpreting it. Prayer expressed in physical movement or posture may prove fruitful in offering their *whole* being to God. Learning to let go, let be and let God may help INTJs experience his active presence amid the spontaneity and disorder of life here and now.

When INTJs succumb to stress, perhaps through outer pressures cramping inner space, **Inferior Se** may crudely overtake them. INTJs' intellectual vitality may give way to mindless TV-watching or obsessive cleaning. Self-discipline may slide into sensual indulgence, from over-eating to over-spending, succeeded by blaming others or berating themselves. At such times INTJs need to have their feelings accepted, to let go of duties and details and regain their objective perspective, free from well-meaning advice.

INTJs' **Dominant Ni** is supported by **Auxiliary Extraverted Thinking** (**Te**), enabling them to interact with the outside world. Thinking helps INTJs realize their goals by shaping insights into coherent structures that can be communicated and developed. It also helps INTJs weigh criticism objectively. At its optimum level, thinking harmonizes inspiration with information, identifying opportunities for far-sighted action. Researching and wrestling through complex issues in prayer or discussion, or identifying and taking a stance for justice, may strengthen thinking.

With **Te** underdeveloped, INTJs may withdraw into an inner world of ideas and ideals, becoming unresponsive to outside influences. They may be caught up in a plethora of possibilities with no discrimination between them, or captivated by idiosyncratic notions they cannot convey. They may lose touch with facts or details, with their cutting-edge refusal to accept conventional limitations becoming a stubborn adherence to a personal vision despite outside dissent or contrary evidence.

Where **Auxiliary Te** overshadows **Dominant Ni**, it blocks iNtuition's opportunity to incubate information and ideas, forestalling INTJs' finest inspirations and pushing for premature, inferior decisions and action. Over-active Thinking may also tend towards finding fault in a way that isolates INTJs from those around them as critical observers rather than participants.

At such times, INTJs may use their **Tertiary Feeling** (**F**) to help them consider their impact on others and understand where they may ruffle feathers. It can enable them to be receptive to other perspectives, gain co-operation and integrate with groups. Learning to listen – to feelings as well as content – without evaluating, could foster this function. It may help INTJs engage with their own emotional life, and focus on what to appreciate in others, rather than what to critique. This approach is also reflected in warm prayers of praise, or in shared intercession for others that involves openness to the flow of divine compassion.

ISTP	I	*Aux:* Se	*Dom:* Ti	P
	E	*Ter:* N	*Inf:* Fe	J

> *Whatever your task, put yourselves into it, as done for the Lord and not for your masters, since you know that from the Lord you will receive the inheritance as your reward.* (Colossians 3.23, 24, NRSV)

Journeying to wholeness for ISTPs means affirming their **Dominant Introverted Thinking** (Ti) gifts for incisive analysis and efficient action. It involves celebrating their graceful sensory and physical attunement to their surroundings. ISTPs approach their spiritual life with common-sense practicality, with their capacity for concentration leading them into fruitful contemplation amid their daily tasks, or into dialogue with Jesus alongside them. They may also reflect on how to apply biblical principles, so they embody their faith in tangible experience and walk the talk as they serve others in practical ways.

ISTPs' **Inferior Extraverted Feeling** (Fe) can help them nurture their interpersonal relationships, appreciate others' feelings and learn to express their own, build rapport by seeking to affirm others rather than correct them, and acknowledge the impact of their decisions on others. It may also enable ISTPs to integrate a respect for social structures.

ISTPs may regard Feeling as marginal to the main issue, but Jesus took time to foster personal and social relationships. His use of hospitality's rituals to communicate an acceptance of others set the stage for some dramatic outcomes. Zacchaeus took significant practical steps in putting his life to rights after Jesus affirmed this 'sinner's' worth by choosing to become his guest.[8]

Attending corporate worship that invites participation and emphasizes unity with God and one another may foster this function. The discipline of belonging to a fellowship group that shares personal needs and prays together may also help. ISTPs may find meeting a trusted Christian friend, with whom they can be vulnerable, a good starting point, despite the less familiar agenda of spiritual receptivity rather than physical activity.

If ISTPs succumb to stress, perhaps through disrespect of their space or others' emotional onslaught, negative **Fe** may rear up. ISTPs' clear logic may disintegrate into chaotic emotionalism and wild assumptions of others' hostility. Eruptions of anger, distress or self-pity may give way to embarrassment at lack of self-control. ISTPs then need personal space, free of duties or pressure to disclose their emotions. Regaining a calmer mindset will help them ground themselves and acknowledge their own emotional life.

ISTPs' **Dominant Ti** is supported by **Auxiliary Extraverted Sensing (Se)**, connecting them to the outer world by feeding a constant flow of factual data for thinking to process and channel into action. It enables ISTPs to move out into new experiences. At its optimum level, Sensing equips ISTPs to make appropriate, effective decisions. Activities that stimulate the senses, such as a prayer-walk in the woods or making something beautiful for God, from a loaf of bread to a clay sculpture, may nurture this function.

With **Se** underdeveloped, ISTPs will lack sufficient grounds on which to make sound decisions. Their avenue to the outer world may become tenuous, leading to greater protectiveness of their own space and heightened, unsubstantiated fears of it being taken over. ISTPs may draw back from new experiences, become isolated from the world at large and stay within an enclave of the like-minded. Their tendency to procrastinate about making decisions will be inflamed.

When **Auxiliary Se** crowds out **Dominant Ti**, ISTPs may fall prey to a multi-sensory overload that leaves them with scant time to evaluate, discern and prioritize. The result may be poorly formulated decisions, based on an immediate response to Sensing's lead, and which may seem haphazard rather than cogent and logical. When Thinking loses out in this way, ISTPs' achievements will suffer.

At such times, ISTPs may draw on their **Tertiary iNtuition (N)** to see a situation from a different angle and access fresh possibilities. ISTPs' dependence on facts may be supplemented by iNtuition's creative vision, introducing wisdom from the unconscious to conscious common sense. iNtuition may take ISTPs beyond immediate preoccupations to consider longer-term factors and consequences. Dreaming dreams, following wherever the Spirit prompts through inner hunches, and brainstorming ideas with others, may all help ISTPs let go their hold on practical details and let God take charge.

ISFP	I ⎡ *Aux:* Se *Dom:* Fi ⎤ P
	E ⎣ *Ter:* N *Inf:* Te ⎦ J

Rejoice in the Lord always. I will say it again: Rejoice! Let your gentleness be evident to all.   (Philippians 4.4–5)

Journeying towards wholeness for ISFPs involves affirming their **Dominant Introverted Feeling (Fi)** gift of tender care for the well-being of all God's Creation. It means celebrating their perceptive awareness and joy of life's fullness in the present moment. ISFPs cherish freedom to wander on the Way according to their unique personal rhythm and the Holy Spirit's leading. They overflow in thankful, heartfelt prayer, often on the move, in response to God's goodness. Shared prayer for others' healing, perhaps with laying on of hands or anointing with oil, may also resource ISFPs and bless those around them.

ISFPs' **Inferior Extraverted Thinking (Te)** can help them reach closure, or impose limits on others' demands, to preserve their room for manoeuvre and protect them from exploitation or exhaustion. Impersonal Thinking may help ISFPs acknowledge others' weaknesses and, conversely, their own strengths, as well as deal with criticism constructively.

ISFPs may react against Thinking's logical decision-making, but it may sometimes be the right approach. When the disciples tracked down Jesus at prayer to tell him the people in Capernaum sought him, his response was to move on. This decision may have seemed unkind, but Jesus' mission involved the wider proclamation of his coming. He was not swayed by pleasing people in the short term, but kept faithful to God's long-term strategy of salvation.[9]

The discipline of prayer at set times may enable ISFPs to balance their lives with some order, while issue-based Bible study may help them clarify principles apart from any compulsion of personal considerations. As they patiently apply their minds, ISFPs may find pure new insights breaking through the clouds of complexity. Discussion with others may also teach them valuable skills in articulating and asserting their own values.

When ISFPs fold under stress, perhaps through facing harsh disrespect of their sensitivities, undeveloped Te may gain mastery. ISFPs may become critical and nitpicking of others and, eventually, themselves. Fearful forebodings may panic them into grasping at control through precipitous, ill-judged action. At such times, reasoning may prove fruitless: ISFPs need others' simple acceptance of their negative feelings to help them recover their openness to new possibilities and facts, and regain a healthier perspective.

ISFPs' **Dominant Fi** is supported by **Auxiliary Extraverted Sensing (Se)**. This supplies factual information for ISFPs to process through their personal values filter, and presents opportunities for appropriate action. At its optimum level, Sensing eases the tension between ISFPs' inner aspirations and life's outer constraints. It provides the raw material for their common sense and experience to work on, devising fresh solutions that bypass the obstacles. Exploring activities that demand attention to detail may foster Sensing, as will seeking God's presence in *all* things – even those that bring pain rather than joy.

With Se underdeveloped, limited input will lead to ISFPs' outlook becoming rigid and self-protective, their values paralysed into inaction. Sensing will confirm existing prejudices, rather than suggest new possibilities through a more inclusive garnering of information. Making narrow decisions on flimsy evidence, ISFPs may cling stubbornly to their viewpoint, interpreting anything less than direct support as a personal attack.

However, when **Auxiliary Se** overrides **Dominant Fi**, the space ISFPs need to maintain their connection with their inner still point will be crushed by an information overload. This will impact on their decisions: ISFPs need reflective time to appraise their perceptions and reach their best conclusions. With no opportunity for this, ISFPs may avoid decision-making altogether, letting other people or circumstances take over.

At such times, ISFPs' **Tertiary iNtuition (N)** can enable them to rise above the detail and glimpse a more overarching vision. iNtuition can free ISFPs from present deadlock by bringing into play the future factor and the longer-term ramifications of decisions. Listening to dreams or exploring signs and symbols in poetic or prophetic writings may nudge ISFPs into new territory. Praying large-scale visionary prayers rather than focusing on current minutiae may also facilitate ISFPs' creative shift of attention from details to destiny.

INFP	I	*Aux:* Ne	*Dom:* Fi	P
	E	*Ter:* S	*Inf:* Te	J

And we know that in all things God works for the good of those who love him, who have been called according to his purpose.
(Romans 8.28)

INFPs resonate with the journey towards personal wholeness, as their **Dominant Introverted Feeling (Fi)** seeks congruence between their aspirations and achievements, and inner harmony of heart, mind and soul. Such a journey means affirming their integrity and ingenuity, and celebrating their compassionate heart for others, whom they help and heal on their way. INFPs need to live out of a felt sense of God's caring presence. The primacy of prayer – possibly in a small group, but certainly in silence and alone – is a *sine qua non*. They may treasure space to enjoy God at depth, and discern the Holy Spirit's nudgings through hunches and dreams.

INFPs' **Inferior Extraverted Thinking (Te)** can encourage a more objective and strategic view in their values-based decision-making, and offset their tendency to be so consumed by the personal that they ignore any wider considerations. It may help them respond constructively to criticism and face conflict dispassionately, so they can tackle the issues rather than become overwhelmed and self-blaming.

INFPs may recoil from 'cold' Thinking principles as signifying an uncaring response, but when the rich young man was crestfallen at the challenge to renounce his worldly wealth, Jesus 'looked at him and loved him',[10] without rushing to renegotiate more lenient terms. Rather, he gave the man freedom to make his choice and experience the consequences.

Participating in a Bible study group focused on theological analysis will stretch INFPs to develop their thinking function, as will interceding with others around political or structural matters.

Debating may help INFPs be more assertive about their values, areas of disagreement or critical appraisal. Thinking judgement can deepen INFPs' wisdom as they consider the long-term implications of decisions, not just the immediate felt impact.

Under severe stress, perhaps through becoming a martyr to their ideals at their own emotional expense, INFPs' **Inferior Te** may erupt in negative ways. They may become angry, unsparing fault-finders, riding roughshod over others' feelings in uncharacteristically bossy behaviour. As they slide into self-criticism, INFPs may need time to regain equilibrium, aided by emotional support rather than reasoned arguments. Ultimately, they may learn to be kinder to themselves, and more realistic about their negative potential and positive strengths.

INFPs' **Dominant Fi** is supported by **Auxiliary Extraverted iNtuition (Ne)**, tuned to perceive underlying meanings, connections and possibilities for humanity. INFPs sift its harvest of insights and impressions using their feeling values, to discern and select what they judge worth keeping and formulate ways of directing this into creative ways of serving others. At its optimum level, iNtuition helps INFPs resolve the tension they can feel between the rock of inner vision and the hard place of outer action.

With **Ne** underdeveloped, INFPs' decisions become based on minimal input. They may then try to force unrealistic expectations on a situation. Alternatively, they may become trapped into in-activity by their idealism, knowing neither where to start nor how to finish what can never be good enough. iNtuition can unlock this paralysis of perfectionism by opening up a flow of information to suggest new avenues. Exploring symbols in art and worship, and musing on imaginative possibilities in the situations around them, may foster this function.

Where **Auxiliary Ne** overtakes **Dominant Fi**, the individual space INFPs need to reflect and refine their values to make their best deci-sions becomes pushed out. Captivated by curiosity, they become full of interesting ideas and successive experiences but directionless, through being starved of engagement with their personality's heart.

INFPs' **Tertiary Sensing (S)** may balance the impressions they absorb with concrete information about practical realities: some-times the dreamer needs to be fed as well as the dream! Gaining a more inclusive picture of a situation may ground INFPs in discern-ing how to act more effectively in realizing their ideals. Attending to material details about available resources, praying about specifics and undertaking measurable activities may help INFPs organize and actually complete the job in hand rather than yearn towards a misty future.

INTP	I ⎡ *Aux:* Ne *Dom:* Ti ⎤ P
	E ⎣ *Ter:* S *Inf:* Fe ⎦ J

> *I keep asking that the God of our Lord Jesus Christ, the glorious Father, may give you the Spirit of wisdom and revelation, so that you may know him better.* (Ephesians 1.17)

Journeying to wholeness for INTPs means celebrating their **Dominant Introverted Thinking**'s (Ti) joy in learning, intellectual agility and ability. It involves honouring their creative originality in using knowledge as a stepping-stone towards deeper understanding and a clearer perception of principles. Theological speculation and rigorous discussion of truth, as well as extensive, sacrosanct space for solitary prayer and self-examination, may foster INTPs' growth in spiritual wisdom. Their praying, often conceptual and contemplative in nature, may also be enhanced via cogent structures of worship or prayer they judge as consistent with truth.

INTPs' **Inferior Extraverted Feeling** (Fe) may help them engage with a relational, rather than rational, approach, and enlighten them as to the potential personal impact of their actions. It can soften impatience towards others' logical inconsistencies, and offset INTPs' tendency to critique motives rather than affirm worth.

INTPs may downplay Feeling's social and emotional aspects of living, yet these can powerfully express human unity. The Pharisees berated Jesus for partying with those of dubious social and religious acceptability, but this was not time-wasting indulgence.[11] Rather, it revealed a truth about the Kingdom of Heaven, which Jesus depicted as a banquet: a celebratory occasion embracing all who respond to God's inclusive invitation.[12]

Engaging with others, through socializing or in caring tasks, can help INTPs connect. The experience of shared, affective prayer and worship may also be fruitful. By applying their desire to learn to others' feelings, views and concerns, INTPs may foster Feeling, and also develop the ability to communicate in person-centred, rather than abstract, language. Thus their own insights may become more widely accessible.

Under great stress, perhaps through inconsiderate invasion of their personal space, wayward **Inferior Fe** may overthrow INTPs. Characteristically calm, they may be embarrassed to find themselves overwhelmingly angry or tearful, self-pitying or accusatory towards others' perceived lack of care. At such times, asking them how they are feeling may only exacerbate things. INTPs need space to reflect, modify their perspective, regain personal trust and accept their own illogical, though real, emotional vulnerability.

INTPs' **Dominant Ti** is supported by **Auxiliary Extraverted iNtuition (Ne)**. This outer-oriented function feeds curious-minded INTPs with material for analysis and exploration. It also enhances their Thinking ability with quickness, ingenuity and subtlety. iNtuition can help INTPs observe principles regarding others' sensitivities, even if they do not feel them. It may also suggest creative ways of communication. At its optimum level, iNtuition's wide-ranging receptivity provides INTPs with a wealth of data and experience from which to learn.

With insufficiently developed **Ne**, INTPs can become isolated, cut off from new knowledge and experience. Their focus may narrow down to only what seems directly relevant to immediate concerns. Too little fuel for thought leads to unproductive conclusions, with significant factors overlooked or rejected: wider interaction furnishes INTPs with more expansive foundations for thinking. Willingness to venture beyond the horizons of personal control or specialist interest, and to scan the world for meaning with greater objectivity, will nurture iNtuition.

Where **Auxiliary Ne** swamps **Dominant Ti**, INTPs may be endlessly stimulated by successive insights, but unable to integrate their material into a cogent intellectual whole. INTPs always face tension between reaching a satisfactory conclusion versus the need for revision through the influx of more information. A continuing plethora of new data blocks the achievement of even a basic working theory, let alone one that can be developed.

Drawing on their **Tertiary Sensing (S)** may offer INTPs a reality check: Sensing's input may seem too obvious to merit INTPs' attention, but reckoning with factual limitations may spare them wasted energy on pursuing impossibilities. Since INTPs tend to live in the mind rather than the body, engaging the senses in action that demands attention to practical detail or physical movement may be therapeutic. Prayer earthed in day-to-day situations, including sensual stimulation such as music or colour, may add substance to worship. INTPs may also benefit from praising God for things as they are now, rather than critiquing what falls short of the ideal.

ESTP	E ⎡ *Dom:* Se *Aux:* Ti ⎤ P
	I ⎣ *Inf:* Ni *Ter:* F ⎦ J

> *Faith by itself, if it is not accompanied by action, is dead.*
> *(James 2.17)*

Journeying towards wholeness for ESTPs means celebrating their energy for life in all its fullness here and now. It involves affirming their **Dominant Extraverted Sensing's (Se)** sharp sensual alertness to their surroundings, and swift and effective action in response. ESTPs grow as they express faith in deeds that minister to those around them: spiritual life becomes real when enfleshed in practical action, perhaps accompanied by short prayers throughout the day, rather than in an extended quiet time. Hymns, set prayers and Bible passages may help ESTPs structure their personal devotions, alongside the stimulus of shared spontaneous worship.

ESTPs' **Inferior Introverted iNtuition (Ni)** can introduce them to perspectives beyond the present, and highlight fresh possibilities. It can help them realize there may be more to a situation than meets the physical eye, encouraging them to interpret information rather than merely absorb it. It may also help them glimpse the bigger picture and develop more strategic vision.

ESTPs may regard iNtuition's perspective as insubstantial, but Jesus urged his disciples to see this world's physical reality in the light of the Kingdom to come. The disciples were not merely to observe events, but to interpret their significance in terms of God's unfolding long-term plan, and so face them with faithful confidence rather than fearful confusion.[13]

Making time for inner reflection, slowing down the pace towards stillness, may help ESTPs nurture iNtuition. As they sit, quietly aware of God's presence and resting with what comes up from within rather than wrestling with what comes in from without, their patience may be tested. Such prayerful, open-ended musing may not produce immediate results, but like a seed planted underground, fruition emerges from unseen growth.

If ESTPs succumb to stress, perhaps through being trapped by routine or commitments, immature **Inferior Ni** may overpower them. ESTPs may read signs of personal criticism or hostility in others' behaviour. Their optimism may sink under vague imaginings of impending doom, as they withdraw under a cloud of conspiracy theories. ESTPs may need reassurance to help them regain their realism, rediscover room for manoeuvre, and learn to accept aspects of the unknown without feeling threatened.

ESTPs' **Dominant Se** is supported by **Auxiliary Introverted Thinking** (Ti), enabling them to analyse information logically to assess their next move. It can bring stability, grounding ESTPs in a rationale for action, not just a race for achievement. It can help them set priorities, complete projects and be tough where needed. At its optimum level, Thinking enables ESTPs to integrate direct action with lasting principles. Consulting Scripture to test their actions against its truth, however uncomfortable or complex and whatever the implications or applications, may foster Thinking.

With **Ti** underdeveloped, ESTPs will lack discrimination amid an abundance of sensory input. Over-reliant on their ability to 'think on their feet', their decisions may become wayward, founded on shallow, impulsive responses. They may struggle to set a direction or hold themselves to account. The thrill of exploring life's funfair of sensory experiences may come at the cost of personal consistency and determination.

When **Auxiliary Ti** overrides **Dominant Se**, ESTPs' adaptability may diminish, since their decisions will be confined to the most immediately accessible information. Their actions may narrow down to satisfying a personal appetite for physical challenge. As Thinking crowds out Sensing's rich potential, ESTPs may also become unduly harsh towards others through inattention to their presentation.

ESTPs may then draw on their **Tertiary Feeling** (F) to attune to how other people experience their actions. Their tough love can be offset by more tender care and a willingness to put appreciative feelings into words, not just deeds. Feeling can help ESTPs honour people's dignity, rather than rate their usefulness. Sharing their own feelings, and allowing others to reveal vulnerability without fear of being crushed by ESTPs' buoyant one-upmanship may foster growth in this area, as will gently holding people before God in prayer. Exploring personal relationships can challenge ESTPs in a new way.

ESFP	E	*Dom:* Se	*Aux:* Fi	P
	I	*Inf:* Ni	*Ter:* T	J

Taste and see that the LORD is good.

(Psalm 34.8)

Moving towards wholeness for ESFPs involves celebrating their **Dominant Extraverted Sensing (Se)** joy in God's world and optimistic disposition towards life in all its fullness. It means affirming their ability to bring smiles to people's faces as they minister to practical needs with generosity, ingenuity and energy. ESFPs' straightforward faith is enlivened by engaging with God 'on the go'. They may need to recognize that prayer is expressed as much in their actions as in the words they use when praying aloud with others. Sensory stimuli such as visual aids or music may also help ESFPs participate in worship with their whole being.

ESFPs' **Inferior Introverted iNtuition (Ni)** can provide a creative counter-balance to their focus on the details of the moment. ESFPs may need to widen their vision, get in touch with the meaning behind the matter, and catch sight of life as not just a succession of events but a sequence that harbours underlying connections.

Party-going ESFPs need to remember that even the sociable Jesus spent time alone in intimate companionship with his Father. Jesus' Gethsemane prayers reveal his capacity to face deep inner turmoil and come to terms with making his great sacrificial act on the Cross for the sake of the ultimate big picture – the future possibility of salvation for all.[14]

Making space for quiet reflection and praying about potential, not just immediate realities, can be fruitful for ESFPs, who may need to offset their drive to be doing with the blessing of being. Resting patiently in God rather than rushing onwards may be therapeutic and creative. iNtuition may also enable ESFPs to open up feared no-go areas of ambiguity or anxiety, and gain courage to see something through rather than run away.

When ESFPs' spontaneous activity is pinned down and pressurized by constricting structures, **Inferior Ni** may erupt in a negative expression. Wide-ranging optimism is overtaken by narrow-focused pessimism and fears for self or loved ones. Lost in inner confusion, ESFPs may become hypersensitive, misinterpret others' intentions and obsess over all-embracing theories of doom. Others' gentle input may help to reintroduce a realistic perspective on feared possibilities, and support ESFPs in discerning their priorities.

ESFPs' **Dominant Se** is supported by **Auxiliary Introverted Feeling** (**Fi**), helping them to set an effective direction based on underlying values. It enables them to combine compassionate desires and factual information in responsible action, and to choose what they wish to bring to life rather than simply going with the flow. At its optimum level, Feeling helps ESFPs keep faith with their better selves and higher purposes. Engaging in empathic intercession and taking time to cultivate close relationships with significant others may nurture Feeling.

If **Fi** is insufficiently developed, ESFPs may lose their grounding and impulsively flit from one experience to another. Their unfettered Sensing may opt for the love of a good time, resisting outer constraints. Feeling provides an inner code of standards and sense of self-worth, helping ESFPs withstand temptations to over-indulge themselves or give in to others' demands.

Where **Auxiliary Fi** overtakes **Dominant Se**, ESFPs' Sensing spontaneity and receptivity may be starved, cramping their ability to learn and improvise in the thick of the action, where they hone skills and gain knowledge. Their decisions will then draw on limited data, trapped within a narrow basis of immediate sensual concerns rather than growing in wisdom.

ESFPs can be enriched by using their **Tertiary Thinking** (**T**) to step back from seeing everything in terms of subjective personal reaction. They may be taxed as they tease out complex moral issues, analyse consequences of actions via reason rather than experience, and reflect on what is theologically consistent rather than practically expedient. However, this process can enable ESFPs to incorporate a long-term dimension to their decision-making: to make plans, set goals, use time efficiently and leave an ongoing legacy to their communities.

ENFP	E ⌈ ***Dom:*** Ne ***Aux:*** Fi ⌉ P
	I ⌊ *Inf:* Si *Ter:* T ⌋ J

I have become all things to all people, so that I might by any means save some. I do it all for the sake of the gospel, so that I may share in its blessings. (1 Corinthians 9.22, 23, NRSV)

Journeying towards wholeness for ENFPs involves them in much-loved celebration – of their **Dominant Extraverted iNtuition's** (Ne) joyful involvement in all life's possibilities for discovery and inspiration. It means affirming their empathy for others and enthusiasm in envisioning them to fulfil their potential. ENFPs grow as they pursue an authentic spiritual life, given impetus through spiritual and scriptural exploration in discussion with others. They thrive as encouragers, sharing others' joys and sorrows and offering heartfelt care and prayer. ENFPs may also forge fruitful relationships through liaising between groups inside and outside church circles.

ENFPs' **Inferior Introverted Sensing** (Si) can offset their idealistic tendency to shoot into the stratosphere by anchoring them in a project's objective facts and practical details, current reality and past experience. It can make ENFPs aware of their own physical needs and avoid the relentless activity that leads to exhaustion. It may foster a more focused receptivity and reflection.

ENFPs may discount the 'ordinariness' of Sensing, but Jesus affirmed its value at the Last Supper as he commanded his disciples to break bread and drink wine in remembrance of him.[15] The call to savour and remember through the discipline of a repeated ritual can keep us grounded in faith's foundations.

Fostering bodily awareness through paying attention to inner feelings and sensations, perhaps in acts of deliberate relaxation or meditation, may help ENFPs develop Sensing and bring them back to themselves. They may benefit from a methodical pattern of prayer. ENFPs may also find that making something, from a meal to a garment, that involves slowing down and following instructions, will allow their ingenuity to lie fallow for a time.

When ENFPs succumb to stressful exhaustion, perhaps from over-extending themselves in too many directions, negative **Inferior Si** may overpower them. ENFPs will lose energy as their openness to possibilities shrinks down to tunnel vision. They may become withdrawn and fixated on small details – perhaps misinterpreting one physical symptom as an indication of serious illness. ENFPs then need low-key support, with space to experience and reflect on their inner state. Once recovered, they may readjust their lifestyle to take more account of their own needs.

ENFPs' **Dominant Ne** is supported by **Auxiliary Introverted Feeling (Fi)**. This enables them to evaluate their inspirations and set priorities. It helps them gain the motivation to see a project through to completion, so that what they perceive, they can achieve. At its optimum level, Feeling helps ENFPs balance their need for outer acceptance with the call to keep faith with their inner values. Listening for others' feelings and allowing them to touch their own emotional life may foster this function.

With **Fi** underdeveloped, ENFPs will have limited capacity to discriminate between their wealth of ideas. Confusing judgement with being judgemental, ENFPs will try to remain all-accepting, and become vulnerable to deception or risky sensation-seeking. They may move from one person or project to the next, seeking the spectacular, with little self-discipline in holding to a consistent course. They may neglect primary loyalties for grander causes, or offer ill-timed insights to others.

Where **Auxiliary Fi** overtakes **Dominant Ne**, ENFPs' creativity may be curtailed through taking in insufficient information. They may experience diminished confidence in their own insights, and take others' perceptions on board too quickly. This loss of their unique vision makes ENFPs of less service to others. They may also find themselves making impetuous decisions based on deeply held values with limited awareness of the implications.

At such times, ENFPs may fruitfully use their **Tertiary Thinking (T)** to enable them to assess their insights and intentions logically, and weigh the long-term consequences beyond immediate personal impact. Thinking can help ENFPs respond to criticism dispassionately, without over-reacting to it as a personal attack, and deal with conflict more constructively. Applying their minds to wrestling with complex issues, and staying with uncomfortable feelings and unpleasant truths can foster Thinking, teaching ENFPs that creative possibilities can emerge from unexpected places.

ENTP	E	*Dom:* Ne	*Aux:* Ti	P
	I	*Inf:* Si	*Ter:* F	J

Forget the former things; do not dwell on the past. See, I am doing a new thing! Now it springs up; do you not perceive it?

(Isaiah 43.18, 19)

Moving towards wholeness for ENTPs means celebrating the impetus they offer in the journey towards God's glorious coming Kingdom, and the fulfilment of creative potential this could realize. It involves affirming their **Dominant Extraverted iNtuition**'s (**Ne**) gift in pointing out new horizons, as they glimpse tomorrow's possibilities that defy today's limitations. ENTPs' iNtuition is nourished in wide-ranging, spontaneous prayer exploring complex issues and creative alternatives with no set conclusion in mind. Worship incorporating variety and challenge may help. Unsettledness can make them self-critical of their spiritual life.

ENTPs' **Inferior Introverted Sensing (Si)**, a selective mode of perceiving based in current material reality, can offer an anchor-point to ENTPs' impulsive pull towards the future possibilities. ENTPs may experience such a focus as limiting, but it can help them maintain personal well-being through realistic choices based on life here and now rather than in the wide blue yonder.

Jesus' earthly mission generated amazing cosmic and eternal consequences, yet amid the crowds pressing in on him on his way, he remained alert to the moment via his senses. When one particular woman touched him for healing from haemorrhage problems, Jesus felt it and reacted instantly, responding with a one-to-one conversation and blessing.[16]

Patiently attending to the tangible detail of one practical task rather than chasing after multiple projects can be restorative for ENTPs. Physicality can be important: ENTPs may lose touch with their bodies as their minds fire off into theoretical realms, and become unaware where they are over-extending themselves. Quiet, sense-oriented activities such as painting or gardening, that offer opportunity to pause and tune in to their senses again, can help ENTPs regain stability.

Where ENTPs do over-tire themselves, **Inferior Si** may flare up negatively. These previously expansive personalities may become enmeshed in preoccupation with minute details, and obsess over what they would not formerly have noticed. Their ability to generate possibilities slips away, and with it, their energy. Space to reflect and low-key pastoral support can enable them to re-engage their thinking and direct it towards their personal welfare rather than global concerns.

ENTPs' **Dominant Ne** is supported by **Auxiliary Introverted Thinking** (Ti), which helps them shape their welter of schemes and dreams logically around clear organizing principles. Formulating models and determining appropriate rationales for action helps ENTPs capitalize on their insights, rather than surfing impulsively from one idea to the next. Effectively developed, this decision-making function can lead to powerful outcomes for ENTPs' visionary and inventive enterprises.

With **Ti** underdeveloped, ENTPs may be strong in inspirations, but weak in implications. Lacking due regulation or evaluation, they may pour out their resources indiscriminately into too many projects. Thinking can bring closure; options are pruned for the sake of fruitfulness. A tenuous inner compass of values may also lead to over-dependence on others' response – even if ENTPs express that by rebelling against others' expectations. Tackling the inward rather than the outward challenge through developing a discipline of meditation may strengthen this function for ENTPs. Painstaking examination of priorities in the presence of God and his word may also help.

Where ENTPs' **Auxiliary Ti** overrides **Dominant Ne**, the wealth of stimuli and information they feed on to foster their creativity and prescience is curtailed. If their fluid intelligence is frog-marched towards premature conclusions, ENTPs' perceptive abilities may be hobbled, resulting in off-beam insights. Wisdom emerges from the *balance* of experience and evaluation.

ENTPs may cultivate such balance in their decision-making by drawing on their **Tertiary Feeling** (F). Feeling can enable them to consider the human factors in situations: appreciating others for who they are as well as what they contribute; adapting proposals or limiting behaviour in the light of their impact on those around them. Without it, ENTPs may tend towards harshness, through becoming isolated from their own feelings and those of others. Acts of practical kindness, not least in attentive listening to others' feelings, may foster this dimension, as may prayer expressing their own feelings to God.

| ESTJ |

E ⎰ *Aux:* Si   *Dom:* Te ⎱ J
I ⎱ *Ter:* N   *Inf:* Fi ⎰ P

> *For we are what he has made us, created in Christ Jesus for good works,*
> *which God prepared beforehand to be our way of life.*
>
> *(Ephesians 2.10, NRSV)*

Journeying towards wholeness for ESTJs involves celebrating their dedicated offering of thoroughly organized and competently executed acts of practical service. It means affirming their **Dominant Extraverted Thinking's (Te)** clarity of analysis, directness and integrity. ESTJs sustain their devotional life through disciplined attendance at corporate worship, underlining their solidarity with the faith community and loyalty to its traditions. Their firm-mindedness is evident in their willingness to pose challenging questions that can put the faithful on the spot. Yet ESTJs are also unflinching in calling themselves to account over their personal moral consistency in Christian discipleship.

ESTJs' **Inferior Introverted Feeling (Fi)** can draw their attention to the personal values their logical predisposition may miss. Principles may sometimes appropriately give way to considerations of an action's personal impact. But mercy need not lead to mayhem! Feeling may also help ESTJs build personal relationships beyond working alliances, and stay tuned to their own emotional life.

ESTJs may think individual concerns are *ipso facto* subject to the greater good of maintaining social order, but overriding established practice may sometimes be what's needed. When Jesus met the Samaritan woman at the well, he asked her for water, conversed and responded to her questions before revealing his insight into her chequered past. The whole community was eventually touched from this one personal connection.[17]

Learning to listen, to express warmth and appreciate rather than critique others' contributions, may enable ESTJs nurture Feeling. Exploring spontaneous prayer from the heart – perhaps in private at first – may also help. Bible study that focuses on forging a personal connection with Jesus, the Living Word, rather than on impersonal truth, may enable ESTJs to foster a relationship with God for his own sake.

When ESTJs succumb to stress, perhaps through logic's failure to manage their own or others' emotional needs, primitive **Inferior Fi** may erupt. ESTJs may become angry or weepy – states usually avoided as signifying loss of control. They may wrap themselves in the martyr's flag, vehemently complain of being unappreciated, and then withdraw. At such times, gentle talk with others may help ESTJs find words for their intense emotions. As they regain their foothold on factual reality, they may find new respect for humanity and its limitations.

ESTJs' **Dominant Te** is supported by **Auxiliary Introverted Sensing (Si)**, which supplies concrete information to facilitate decisions well-grounded in current realities. ESTJs' retentive factual memory means they can amass an extensive reservoir of knowledge and experience. At its optimum level, Sensing helps ESTJs draw on this to make strategic and subtle judgements, via a truly objective appraisal of facts and variables. Doing something that demands attention to detail, such as a craft activity, or praying with objects such as candles or a cross, may enhance Sensing.

With **Si** underdeveloped, ESTJs may become rigid and impatient, sticking to known procedures and refusing to broaden their outlook through new information. They may become dogmatic, self-proclaiming experts, demanding complete conformity to the party line, and dispensing categorical criticisms of those who deviate from it. They may reject others' input, summarily dismissing whatever fails to meet their definition of rational sense. Those judged as incompetent may feel the sting of ESTJs' expressed impatience.

Where **Auxiliary Si** crowds out **Dominant Te**, however, ESTJs may be overwhelmed with a multiplicity of data they cannot evaluate effectively. In such cases, their decisions are likely to become contrary or severe.

Drawing on their **Tertiary iNtuition (N)** can help ESTJs focus on the bigger picture rather than the immediate detail. The best decisions incorporate iNtuition's awareness of wider consequences, not just Sensing's perception of results here and now. iNtuition may help ESTJs play with possibilities beyond their beloved standard operating procedures. Exploring new forms of worship, particularly meditative prayer, may nurture iNtuition. Responding to the Holy Spirit's nudgings to risk following a prayerful hunch rather practical reason could also open up new territory. ESTJs could even try introducing some unplanned time for fun into their weekly routine.

ESFJ	E	Aux: Si	Dom: Fe	J
	I	Ter: N	Inf: Ti	P

How very good and pleasant it is when kindred live together in unity!
(Psalm 133.1, NRSV)

Journeying towards wholeness for ESFJs involves celebrating their **Dominant Extraverted Feeling** (Fe) commitment to creating harmony and expressing practical care for all in their circles of involvement. It means affirming their gift of organizing people graciously and effectively to bless others. ESFJs, fuelled by Feeling, are enriched as they enjoy the friendship of God and his people: sharing prayers, testimonies and fellowship, engaging in acts of service together, warmly welcoming the stranger and cherishing the Church through honouring its practices.

ESFJs' **Inferior Introverted Thinking** (Ti) can moderate their intense focus on relatedness to detach from others and gain greater flexibility in decision-making. Freed from any tunnel vision of tradition or undue influence of authority, ESFJs can explore fresh approaches.

Thinking may help ESFJs square up to problems and find new ways through the tension they can feel when their desire to comfort others clashes with their clear sense of right and wrong. ESFJs may feel disassociating from others' feelings is wrong, yet it may sometimes be the more righteous response. When the Pharisees questioned Jesus about paying taxes, to force him into expressing disloyalty either to God or to the Emperor, Jesus' thinking cut incisively through the dilemma: using a coin depicting Caesar's head, he distinguished between but equally affirmed what was lawfully owed to the Emperor and that which belonged to God.[18]

Taking time to muse on logical ways round problems, setting aside the personal standpoint to consider other factors, wrestling with theological complexities and praying with the mind as well as from the heart, may all help ESFJs undergird their love with truth and take the risk of disagreeing with others.

If ESFJs experience severe stress, perhaps through a self-induced overload of responsibilities, primitive Ti may overpower them, and their kindness may degenerate into far-reaching criticism. They may wield crude logic, or compulsively scour self-help books for *the* answer. Becoming aware of their behaviour, ESFJs may sink into self-blame. Healing may come through quiet time with themselves as they are, away from outer demands. A creative activity, such as journal-writing, may gently restore perspective; using favourite set prayers may help them restabilize.

ESFJs' **Dominant Fe** is supported by **Auxiliary Introverted Sensing (Si)**, enabling them to use their personal interactions to gain direct personal experience and information, as they home in on all details related to humanity. Equipped with accurate, observable data, ESFJs shape a rationale and practical strategies to help others, demonstrating acumen about what is appropriate for each person or situation. At its optimum level, Sensing grounds ESFJs in realistic knowledge for people-focused action. Deliberately slowing down to focus on all their senses, perhaps on a meandering walk, and patiently seeking God in everything – even what seems ugly or uncomfortable – may nurture Sensing.

With **Si** underdeveloped, ESFJs draw hasty conclusions on thin evidence. They may become dogmatic, assuming they know what others want and insistent on imposing it. Sensing provides information about current realities and specific situations. Without it, ESFJs risk idealistically over-committing themselves, rather than readjusting their expectations to take proper account of their own needs.

When **Auxiliary Si** overtakes **Dominant Fe**, ESFJs can lose confidence in their ability to be personally decisive in the outer world. Instead, they may adopt others' judgements, seeing themselves only in the mirror of their approval, values or leadership, and hesitant about establishing their own position. They may also become locked into the minutiae of the immediate stimuli around them.

At such times, ESFJs' **Tertiary iNtuition (N)** may help them glimpse the bigger picture. iNtuition's more holistic perspective can soften ESFJs' adherence to the solid tramlines of set procedures and nudge them out towards new possibilities. It can enable them to see the future as having positive potential, rather than being uncertain and therefore negative. Exploring symbols in their worship, abandoning routine prayer lists and following where the Spirit leads, and resting in God's mystery and majesty, may all help ESFJs journey into new territory and find growth beyond their comfort zones.

ENFJ	E [*Aux:* Ni *Dom:* Fe] J
	I [*Ter:* S *Inf:* Ti] P

*'For I know the plans I have for you,' declares the LORD, 'plans to pros-
per you and not to harm you, plans to give you hope and a future.'*
                                                    (Jeremiah 29.11)

ENFJs' passion for helping others to wholeness should not preclude
their own journey. This means celebrating their **Dominant Extraverted Feeling (Fe)** gifts of engaging with people with warmth and
insight and affirming their ability to inspire others, drawing out
their potential and drawing them together in harmony. ENFJs' Feeling is expressed in corporate worship, where their gifts may suit
them to lead as well as participate. ENFJs enjoy a committed and
evolving personal relationship with God through open-hearted
prayer across a broad spectrum of forms, perhaps including healing
prayer with laying on of hands.

ENFJs' **Inferior Introverted Thinking (Ti)** can help them dis-
engage to assess things more objectively, say no to others' unrea-
sonable demands, and achieve a healthier balance of care in their
relationships. It can help them detach without guilt, deal fairly with
criticism and address conflicts. Thinking ensures ENFJs' personal
convictions are grounded on clear, cogent principles.

ENFJs may shun impersonal Thinking, but Jesus affirmed its
value when the Pharisees brought him the woman caught in
adultery. As they tried to trap him into a pronouncement, Jesus
remained detached, writing in the ground. His eventual response
that those without sin should cast the first stone set the woman free
and exposed the Pharisees' true inner motivations.[19]

Taking quiet, reflective time to study God's word and grapple
with its complexities could help ENFJs strengthen Thinking. A willingness to turn the light of its truth on themselves and away from
their focused concern for others may also bring growth. ENFJs may
benefit from integrating a thinking approach into their prayer life,
and learn the value of prayer even when it involves difficult feelings
or personal struggle.

If ENFJs burn out through stress, perhaps through over-
extending themselves for others, negative **Inferior Ti** may erupt.
ENFJs may become pessimistic and hypercritical, and then withdraw, ashamed of their insensitivity. They may compulsively seek

absolute truth, using clumsy, categorical logic. In this state, ENFJs need time to process their thoughts, away from others: they may find it helpful to write a personal journal. Ultimately, they may become able to accept that they alone cannot save the whole world.

ENFJs' **Dominant Fe** is supported by **Auxiliary Introverted iNtuition (Ni)**. This facilitates their understanding of people's motivations and situations. It highlights creative possibilities for others' growth and mutual harmony. At its optimum level, iNtuition breathes the fresh air of new possibilities, challenges and ideas into ENFJs' decision-making. Dreaming dreams, learning to trust hunches, and musing and praying with no particular goal in mind, may strengthen this function. In doing these by themselves, ENFJs may realize the fruitfulness of solitude.

With **Ni** underdeveloped, ENFJs may become locked in their personal convictions. Their desire to settle matters may distort into a drive to hasty conclusions based on inaccurate assumptions. They may confuse their personal values with objective fact and become more insistent on imposing them, perceiving others' viewpoints simply as criticism of their own. They will lose their individual adaptability, lining up rigidly with social rules.

Where **Auxiliary Ni** overruns **Dominant Fe**, ENFJs will be over-stimulated by new ideas and possibilities, but uncertain how to prioritize and organize the wealth of data. They may then make inconsistent or poorly formulated decisions. As self-doubt creeps in, they may resolve their confusion by taking the easy route to instant harmony, and allowing others to decide on their behalf.

At such times, ENFJs may access their **Tertiary Sensing (S)** to remind them of facts and details and ground them on solid foundations. Sensing can reawaken ENFJs' awareness of their physical bodies and concrete realities, taking the heat out of future-focused idealism, and fostering ENFJs' contentment here and now. Engaging in physical activity, and using their senses to enjoy experiences of God's Creation, music, art or good food, may rebalance ENFJs, and help them relax their push to make life better for all. They may then taste the well-being they strive to achieve for others.

ENTJ	E	[	*Aux:* Ni	*Dom:* Te	]	J
	I	[	*Ter:* S	*Inf:* Fi	]	P

Be strong and courageous, because you will lead this people to inherit the land I swore to their forefathers to give them.   *(Joshua 1.6)*

ENTJs' journey into wholeness involves affirming their **Dominant Extraverted Thinking's** (Te) gifts of decisive leadership and abundant energy. It means celebrating their capacity to absorb a mass of impersonal information and their incisive perception of possibilities for change. As natural organizers who love God with their minds, ENTJs' spiritual path may be characterized by order and content. Gaining knowledge about God can resource them and raise challenging issues. ENTJs may wrestle these through in prayerful reasoning and follow up their conclusions with righteous action. Engagement with the written word or face-to-face with an intelligent spiritual guide may be equally stimulating.

ENTJs' **Inferior Introverted Feeling** (Fi) can help them bring their plans to fruition by including a consideration of their impact on those they intend to implement them. ENTJs may be ships' captains, setting ambitious destinations, but their crew need to want to sail with them. ENTJs may also need to touch base with the emotional toll their actions and pace of living take on them personally.

ENTJs may dismiss Feeling as an inadequate basis for decision-making, or even as weakness, but they need to note the part it played in Jesus' ministry. Jesus knew he would bring Lazarus back to life, yet still wept at his tomb. Though his miracle would bring glory to God and foreshadow his own victory over death, Jesus still took time to engage with what Lazarus' loss meant for his loved ones, acknowledging their grief alongside his own.[20]

Learning to listen to others express feelings as well as information, being receptive to their contribution, and offering affirmation and appreciation may oil hidden wheels in ENTJs' relationships. Being willing to accept and explore their own feelings may also foster spiritual wholeness. ENTJs may need safe places to do this: in individual prayer, perhaps, or watching a film alone, talking with a trusted other or playing with children and pets.

Under stress, perhaps through dealing with others expressing irrational feelings, ENTJs tend to sustain their outer performance for a long time, so when they finally fall prey to a destructive surge of **Inferior Fi**, the change seems swift and dramatic. ENTJs may erupt in emotional outbursts, show vulnerability to feeling criticized or undervalued, or lapse into self-pity. In this state they need those they trust to accept and contain these disturbing feelings, and help them talk things out. ENTJs may afterwards reassess their own limits realistically and gain a new appreciation of the value of close relationships.

ENTJs' **Dominant Te** is supported by **Auxiliary Introverted iNtuition** (Ni), which helps ensure their decision-making is adequately informed. iNtuition discerns meanings and connections, possibilities and overall strategies. This unifying process clarifies ENTJs' vision into a cogent whole, from which their decisions for creative change emerge. At its optimum level, iNtuition provides the insight to direct ENTJs' actions into leading others in a creative, courageous direction. Strengthening iNtuition may require patience: 'wasting time' in quiet musing or the passivity of contemplative prayer can be fruitful, especially where the demand for immediate results is relinquished.

Where **Ni** is underdeveloped, ENTJs will make hasty decisions without fully engaging with the issues or exploring the possibilities. Their impatience and upfront strength in driving things along may be experienced as coercive and overbearing.

Where **Auxiliary Ni** overtakes **Dominant Te**, ENTJs may make decisions without the full benefit of their capacity for logical analysis and planning. Their plentiful supply of brilliant insights and ideas may not be thoroughly sifted into considered or consistent decisions.

ENTJs can choose to enrich their resources for making effective decisions by drawing on their **Tertiary Sensing** (S). Sensing may enable ENTJs to absorb factual detail, slowing them down to provide a counter-balance of immediacy for these energetic future-focused types.

Performing a day-to-day task for another, a repetitive physical activity or a country walk with no timetable or goal beyond enjoying the experience of God's Creation, may encourage ENTJs to savour their Sensing.

6

Activities to develop the functions

—•◦•—

Having read your profile in the last chapter, you will now be more familiar with how your particular combination of Myers-Briggs® functions work together. You may already have identified which function(s) you are looking to strengthen or explore. This chapter contains suggested activities for all four functions in both their Extraverted and Introverted expressions for you to use in developing whichever aspects apply to you. The suggestions include both devotional and everyday activities.

Using the suggestions

Our **Dominant** function takes the lead in defining our God-given personality. It is important that this is well developed. If you are, or have been, in circumstances that limit your opportunity to exercise your Dominant, you may wish to focus on activities to strengthen it. So, for example, if your profile is **ESFJ**, work on your Dominant function by exploring the suggestions for **Extraverted Feeling (Fe)**.

Our **Auxiliary** function provides an effective support and balance for our Dominant, without overshadowing it. If reading your profile has alerted you to symptoms of an underdeveloped Auxiliary, you may wish to attend to strengthening this function. So, for example, if your profile is **ISFP**, work on your Auxiliary function by exploring the suggestions for **Extraverted Sensing (Se)**.

Our **Tertiary** function can offer a valuable, balancing perspective. Sometimes it is hard to gain a sense of what our Tertiary actually is, as it is less consciously accessible to us. You may wish to clarify its character and gain some facility in drawing on this function. Since there is some uncertainty about whether we use our Tertiary in an Extraverted or Introverted way, you may find it helpful to explore both sets of suggestions to discern the one that sits more comfortably with you. So, for example, if your profile is **ENFP**, work on your Tertiary function by exploring the suggestions for both **Extraverted** and **Introverted Thinking** (Te and Ti).

The previous chapter's profiles paid significant attention to the **Inferior** function. Since we develop our Dominant function at the expense of our Inferior, the Inferior drops down into our unconscious. Thus, when it does emerge in its undeveloped state, we are less able to handle it constructively, and it is more likely to cause us problems. However, our Inferior can be a rich source of creativity. If you want to become more familiar with your Inferior, so you can use it rather than have it use you, then look at the activities list that matches your Inferior function. Given that you may well be less confident in this area, it is especially important to try these suggestions without any pressure to achieve or succeed. So, for example, if your profile is **INTP**, work on your Inferior by exploring the suggestions for **Extraverted Feeling** (Fe).

It's worth noting that what is the **Dominant** function for ESFJ is INTP's **Inferior**. Four people may be meeting together in a social occasion that requires them using their **Extraverted Feeling** (**Fe**), but whereas one finds this comes naturally, another will be making a great effort to express the same function.

Finally, ensure you focus on one function at a time. Not everything can be developed at once! Besides this, different functions may need strengthening at different times. If you try to do the lot simultaneously, you will end up in confusion and unable to sustain long-lasting growth.

Before we look at some activities, a brief portrait of the *Perceiving* functions may help us identify them more clearly; see Table 7.

Extraverted Sensing (Se)

When we use Extraverted Sensing we are gathering information from the outer world directly via our five senses. We experience and enjoy what is physically around us just as it is, here and now.

1 Take your Bible with you to a favourite spot of nature – from woodland to riverbank – and read Psalm 148 aloud. Enjoy the experience of being surrounded by Creation as you speak out your praises, exhorting heaven and earth to give glory to the living God who has made all things.

Table 7 Perceiving functions

Attitude	Extraverted	Introverted
Sensing	**Se**	**Si**
	Seeks wide-ranging experience of the physical world	Seeks selective experience of the physical world
	Attends to details of present moment	Chooses details from present to store as internal sense impressions
	Enjoys immediate sensory experience	Enjoys relived sensory experience
	Prefers spontaneity and freedom to act	Proceeds methodically and needs limits
	Stimulated by five senses	Attuned to inner sensations
	Enjoys company and action	Enjoys solitude and reflection
iNtuition	**Ne**	**Ni**
	Seeks ideas from outer world	Open to inspiration from inner world
	Brainstorms possibilities for change	Explores possibilities for new understanding
	Optimistic, seeks expanding interests	Mystic, seeks underlying meanings
	Enthusiastic about new ways of doing	Envisioned by new ways of seeing
	Bursts of energy	Hunches emerge from unconscious
	Discusses ideas with others	Ideas remain in intense inner world

2 Read John 15.1–11. Let Jesus' words stay with you as you go into the garden and prune some bushes. Enjoy God's company in the garden. Sense yourself abiding in Jesus, the True Vine, as you tend his Creation. Ask God where he may desire to prune parts of your life for greater fruitfulness, and offer yourself to him. In coming weeks, return to see the new shoots springing forth from your pruning work, and thank God that this is like the fresh growth he is releasing in you.

3 Read Luke 11.2–4, focusing on verse 3: 'Give us each day our daily bread.' Visit your local bakery to buy a loaf – or bake one yourself – enjoying all the smells, sounds and sights of the experience. Cut off a slice, being aware of the feel of the knife cutting through the bread, and eat it. Chew slowly to savour the bread's unique taste and texture. Offer prayers of thanksgiving for God's provision. You may later want to share your loaf with others.

4 Create a 'prayer corner' in a room at home. This might involve choosing objects to place on a small table: a cross, Bible or candle; pine-cone, stone, plant or pot-pourri; a small picture or icon. You may want a sketchpad, musical instrument or the facility to play music close by. You may prefer a prayer-stool or cushion to a chair. Use what you choose to engage your senses and stimulate your faith in the reality of God's presence as you draw close to him in this prayer-dedicated space. You may want to freshen this space by rearranging things or changing your special objects from time to time.

5 Find out one task you can do for someone else that will be of real practical help, and do it. Carry it out as if you were doing it for Jesus himself, making it an active prayer of service and obedience to the Servant King.

6 Seek ways of praying with your body rather than using words. Explore and use different postures to express your praise, confession, loving intercession for others, the bringing of your personal petitions and your self-offering of commitment and obedience.

7 Attend a church service and determine to pay attention to noticing everything going on up at the front and around you at all times, without turning your thoughts inwards to evaluate, ruminate, follow distracting ideas or form opinions on what you experience. Simply devote all your senses to meeting with God in whatever is actually happening, moment by moment.

8 Take an intercessory prayer walk around your local neighbourhood or town, seeking to see what is around you through God's eyes and talking to him about it. Be adventurous and explore one or two roads you have not walked down before. Be open and ready to look with God at the less attractive aspects of your area.

9 Think of the person you love most in the world. Ask yourself how you can see the presence of God in that person. Praise and thank God for what you see, hear and feel. Now think of a person you find difficult to love. Ask God to show you signs of his grace in that person. Don't judge yourself or try to change. Simply allow God's graciousness in you.

10 Look closely at your hand. Feel the texture of your skin and observe all the details: the lines, shape and dimensions, capacity for movement, any marks or unevenness. Give thanks to

God that you are so 'fearfully and wonderfully made'. You may want to try something similar as you study your face in the mirror, remembering that whatever is blemished, you are still cherished – and the same holds true for others' faces, too.

11 Take a long, slow walk round a busy market, using all your senses to absorb your surroundings. Look at the colour, detail, range of wares and positioning of stalls; listen to all the different sounds; if allowed, touch or taste some of the produce. Praise God for what you see, exactly as it is. Try not to analyse or become distracted by speculation: simply stay with what your senses tell you.

12 Cup your hands behind your ears and note the increased intensity of what you can hear. What would it be like to hear at that level all the time? Practise actively listening to, not just hearing, what is around you throughout the day. You may want to extend this practice to your other senses, and focus on seeing, not just looking at; tasting, not just eating; feeling, not just touching; smelling, not just breathing in.

13 Try a new experience that involves your using your senses or engaging in physical activity, e.g. have a party where everyone brings a new dish for others to try; try out a different sport.

14 Make something, from a herb garden to a clay pot. Enjoy the experience of creating with your hands. Be conscious of the feel of whatever material you are working with. Notice textures, colours and smells. Pay close attention to what you are doing, as if this was the only thing that mattered in the world.

15 Observe an animal – perhaps a pet, or animal at a farm or zoo. Notice everything you can about it, and deduce what you can from its appearance, form and behaviour. Take special note of how an animal simply lives in the present moment, and seek to mirror its engagement with what is as you watch patiently.

16 Arrange a bunch of flowers in a vase. Do so slowly, observing the details of each flower, one by one. Notice the differences between them in shape, shade, texture and proportion. Pay particular attention to noticing the distinctions between flowers of the same species.

17 List what happened at a short meeting, incident or other event where you have been present. Make it a list of facts only, without ascribing any meaning, feeling or interpretation to what you describe.

18 Join a dance, exercise, Pilates or yoga class, where you need to pay total attention to bodily movement, stillness or posture. Seek to maintain total concentration on your physical activity.

19 Take time to eat a meal together with family or friends. Stay aware of what is happening in each moment: savour the food and enjoy the company.

20 Choose an ordinary object and focus your attention on observing and experiencing it exactly as it is. Get to know it, using all your senses to notice everything you can about it. At the end of your time, put it out of sight and list everything you noticed about it.

Introverted Sensing (Si)

When we use Introverted Sensing we are selecting information from the outer world via our five senses. We store it internally as a detailed sense impression along with our internal reaction to it. We can then refer to or relive the experience at a later time.

1 Read Psalm 136 slowly and quietly to yourself. Be aware of the repeated refrain, 'For his steadfast love endures for ever' (NRSV), which follows as an affirmation of praise for something God has done as Creator and Deliverer of his people. When you finish the Psalm, speak out or write down things God has done in your own experience and follow each one by declaring 'For his steadfast love endures for ever'.

2 Read Mark 5.24–34 through carefully a few times, and then close your eyes and relive the scene from the woman's perspective. You may draw on your own memories to help you imagine all she is experiencing through her senses: the physical sensations of an unwell body; being in the press of a crowd; a yearning to encounter Jesus and know his healing; the feel of the cloak's material and sensations of bodily well-being. Reflect on what emerges from this meditation, and, like the woman, tell Jesus what has happened to you and receive his response.

3 Read Luke 11.2–4, focusing on the word 'Father'. Think of what it means to have a good father by calling to mind fathers you have known, perhaps including your own. Allow these to help you form a picture of God as the perfect Father in heaven, and spend some time talking to him as his child.

4 Choose a Bible character and follow his or her story through in Scripture. You could select a book centred round a particular person, such as Esther or Ruth, or choose another character and use a Bible dictionary to help you find the references that track the story. Reflect on your character's life and experiences of God. How do God's dealings with them help you in your own faith?

5 Review your day in prayer chronologically, telling Jesus about all its joys and sorrows, and remembering he has been with you through every moment. What memories do you want to treasure? Where do you need to put something right? What occasions have been opportunities to learn, so that recalling them could help you respond differently if the same situation were to recur? Offer Jesus your thanksgivings and receive his forgiveness.

6 Draw a time-line or represent a road or river on a piece of paper and use it to chart your faith-journey. Mark significant dates along the way and add a picture or a few words to remind you of each event. Keep it somewhere safe, so you can use it to encourage you in your prayers. Add to it as new events unfold or you remember other important points. You may wish to show it to a friend and tell them your testimony of God's faithfulness.

7 As you receive bread and wine at a service of Holy Communion, savour the taste and sensation of taking these elements into your body. Reflect on Christ coming into you. What does that feel like? Become aware of how your action links you with believers down the ages, united in obedience to Jesus' instructions at the Last Supper.

8 Sit in a chair in a posture that is relaxed but alert. Close your eyes. Listen to the rhythm of your breathing. Take time to tune in to how you feel in your body right now. Are you conscious of any particular sensations and emotions? As you become aware of anything, gently release it into God's loving care. Let him simply hold your body in being, and note how your sensations and feelings change as you rest in his presence.

9 Create a personal ritual for starting your prayer-time, e.g. lighting a candle, placing a stone by a small cross, repeating a favourite set prayer. Enjoy the way this settling ritual brings you into quiet receptivity to God as you repeat it regularly.

10 Think of one practical act of kindness you could do regularly for a family member, friend or person in need, e.g. a cup of tea when they come in, running a bath, giving a weekly telephone call, picking up a prescription, reading a story. Do this as an expression of ongoing love and care.

11 Take a favourite hymn or one that paints vivid word-pictures (such as 'All Things Bright and Beautiful'), and sing it or read it over to yourself. After each line, picture the scenes and memories it brings to mind and lift them to God in your own words or feelings of praise.

12 Establish a tradition that fosters togetherness among your family, friends or fellowship, e.g. a shared meal on a particular night of the week; a Sunday afternoon walk.

13 When you go to have your hair cut, be aware of the physical sensations you experience on your skin, hair and head as a new shortness and style emerges. Watch the process in the mirror, observing how the change in your appearance makes you feel and look.

14 Visit a place of beautiful surroundings, from gardens to an art gallery. As you wander round, be alert to something particular catching your eye, and then stop to observe more closely in detail. What especially draws you? What associations does it have that reminds you of something similar, or a particular past experience? Enjoy all the aspects of what you are observing through your senses now, and whatever it brings to mind for you.

15 When planning a seasonal family celebration, perhaps birthday or Christmas, recall celebrations of past years. Recall what went well and compare it to what was not so successful. Use this knowledge to plan the occasion this time round.

16 Go to a school reunion or meet with old friends to talk about past times. Compare notes on what you recall as significant activities or occasions, and why they were important. Try to remember events as accurately as you can and note any differences in the details and experience given between your account and those of others. Does this highlight your own personal perspective? Do you, in fact, all remember the same incidents?

17 Recall a particular time when you felt great joy or peace. In your mind's eye, pinpoint exactly where you were, and bring to awareness all the aspects of the scene you can remember, in the

order that they happened. Let your awareness bring to life the emotions and bodily sensations you felt at that time.

18 Use a box or scrapbook to make a collection of things that represent special and significant memories for you. From time to time, come back to it and look through it, using the pictures, objects, cards, letters and so on to prompt your reliving of the events they represent.

19 Take some activity of your everyday living and turn it into a regular routine, from cleaning the bathroom to sorting out paperwork, from doing exercise to reading a book. Note how much less energy it takes to do the activity when it becomes part of an established pattern.

20 Discover the enjoyment and soothing quality of a repeated, rhythmic physical activity, from swimming to knitting, from kneading dough to sanding down a piece of wood.

Extraverted iNtuition (Ne)

When we use Extraverted iNtuition our energy is directed towards the outer world, looking for patterns and connections. We use what we see to generate new options and possibilities for changing things.

1 Read John 21.1–14. Despite their experience and knowledge as fishermen, the disciples ended their night-time expedition frustrated, having failed to make a catch. Be open to how their situation might prompt a connection with any area of activity in your own life. Imagine Jesus alongside, watching your efforts. What would he call out to you? What might it mean, in your situation, to 'fish from the other side', and shift to a radically different approach? Could you risk trying it?

2 Read on through John 21.15–19. Consider Jesus' restoration and commissioning of Peter by a charcoal fire; think back to the night of Jesus' arrest, when Peter denied his Lord by a fire in a Jerusalem courtyard; think forward to Peter's public proclamation of Jesus as Lord in Jerusalem at Pentecost and beyond. How might things have been different had Peter *not* denied Jesus? What new possibilities could emerge from receiving Jesus' forgiveness for times when your own faith has failed? Be open to the Spirit's insights and make your personal response to Jesus' invitation: 'Follow me.'

3 'Your kingdom come, your will be done on earth as in heaven.' What do you see as the characteristics of God's Kingdom? Pray for God's Kingdom rule to break through in the world around you. What would be the evidence of that happening? Envisage actions you could take this week that would be part of the answer to your prayer and carry out at least one of them. Talk to others about what you're doing – you may encourage them to join in!

4 Call to mind a personal situation that has reached deadlock, e.g. a quarrel between friends, an ill relative. Pray for it, imagining yourself alongside the people involved. Using your imagination, move position so it is as if you are looking down on the situation from above the town where it is taking place. What are you aware of now? Pray as you are prompted. Imagine you move further away still, so you are looking down on the country where it is taking place. Again, pray with whatever comes to mind. Move in your imagination again, so it is as if you are looking down on earth from out in space. Pray as you are led. Finally, imagine you come back to where you started, alongside the situation. How do you find yourself praying about it now?

5 Read a selection of articles and stories from a daily newspaper. Can you discern any connections, themes or patterns between them: types of event, viewpoints and values, people's hopes and fears? Reflect on or discuss what you discover, and turn these insights into prayers.

6 Is it harder to find God in the city or in the country? Take a walk in both settings with your spiritual antennae open to things that might connect you with God. What might you discern about the unseen God from what you experience around you? You might want to explore this in other places: an open market, office, sports centre, garden, etc.

7 Reflect on or discuss the different components of a church service or other gathering. How do they relate to one another? Is their order important? What would you want to change, add or take away, and why? Experiment with redesigning the event, to explore the different ways it might fulfil its aims. Or, if you think it necessary, re-create it completely from scratch.

8 Take part in an intercessory prayer group praying for an issue of peace or justice. Since Scripture promises God can do even 'more than we can ask or imagine', release your imagination to

pray bold, ambitious prayers that reflect the strength of your longing for change. Be open to what possibilities such prayers could unleash, not least in suggesting activities for the group itself to follow up.

9 Visit an art gallery with other Christians, and afterwards discuss what you have seen in the light of your faith. What spiritual connections and insights emerge from your experience? Where would you like to question, challenge or affirm the artist(s)?

10 Think of an ongoing prayer request you personally or your church community are making to God. What good might come if your prayer was answered in a different way from what you hope for?

11 Imagine that one object you rely on in your daily routine disappears overnight, e.g. shower, kettle, car. What difference does it make to your day? Imagine ways round the problems created. You may want to try living these out the next day, regardless.

12 Brainstorm as many uses as you can for a domestic object, from a spoon to a TV remote.

13 Go out for a coffee or drink and discreetly observe nearby groups of people or passers-by, noting how they behave towards each other and the relationships between them.

14 Choose a room in your home and consider how you might redesign or redecorate it for the same or another use. Look at the relationship of different zones in the room, and how and where things are positioned. Are there other possibilities? If a total make-over is out of the question, create something different by rearranging objects and furniture.

15 Look at your behaviour patterns round different times of day, e.g. early morning, lunch-time or evening. Could you readjust these to make them more effective in either energizing or calming you? Try changing something in your routine and see if it works better.

16 Think of something you would like to do but have never dared to try because of fear of failure. Determine this will not discourage you, and have a go at the activity. Remind yourself that just daring to do it is a success, regardless of any other outcome.

17 Determine to learn new things during your day: watch a different TV programme (or switch the box off altogether); learn

a new route to work; try a new recipe; find out something new about someone you know or meet regularly.

18 Explore involvement in the expressive arts: from taking a painting course to joining a drama group, or hosting a 'bring and share' music and poetry evening with friends.

19 Read a book or watch a film in the sci-fi or fantasy genre. Discuss how it might have been written or produced differently. What alternative possibilities were there for the story-line? Imagine creating a sequel.

20 Generate as many possibilities as you can for turning one of your leisure interests or voluntary activities into something that earns a living. What would you have to do to make that happen? What would get in the way and how could you overcome the difficulties? You might also want to explore new avenues for using your work skills in a voluntary capacity.

Introverted iNtuition (Ni)

When we use Introverted iNtuition our energy is directed towards the inner world, open to emerging insights and images that reveal underlying meanings not immediately obvious. We gain a vision of how things could be, transformed by new perceptions and perspectives.

1 Read Revelation 1.12–16. Meditate on the figurative language of John's vision of Jesus. Allow his descriptive images to resonate in your spirit, reflecting on their meaning as windows that open up glimpses of the Son of God in his glory. As you envision the transcendent Christ, what images surface to add to John's description? Take time to respond in a silent, adoring gaze of worship.

2 Read Isaiah 43.16–21. Reflect on the paradox that God draws back water to make a pathway through, but also makes water flow in dry places to nourish life. He performed both miracles as he led the Israelites out of Egypt to the Promised Land. Reflect on where, in your journey of faith, God has opened ways through turbulent waters, or brought sustenance in dry places. Let these reflections take you where they will, and when you are ready, turn them to prayer. Re-read verses 18–19 and wait quietly, open to insights about any 'new thing' God might be unfolding in your life.

3 Read Luke 11.2, focusing on 'Father, hallowed be your name.' Without trying to understand or analyse what 'hallowed' means, quietly repeat the phrase in your mind, slowly and in rhythm with your breathing. Gradually come into silence and rest attentively in your hallowed Father's presence. If your mind wanders, gently repeat the phrase till you become settled again. Though this may be difficult to sustain at first, 20 minutes of stillness may be a helpful period to aim for.

4 Practise 'Butterfly Prayer'. Sit in a relaxed but alert position, close your eyes and take some moments to come consciously into God's presence, settling your body and calming your breathing. As you sit, allow thoughts and feelings to surface, and use them as springboards for your prayers, following wherever the Spirit leads.

5 What symbols or images most encapsulate who God is to you? Muse on their significance for you. You may wish to do this by exploring them through drawing, sculpting or writing a poem.

6 Choose a major story in a newspaper. Read it carefully, seeking what may be going on beneath the headlines, within people's lives and the issues involved. What other perspectives could there be on the event? What undercurrents of meaning can you discern? What might the very choice to tell this story represent in today's society? Turn your insights to prayer.

7 When you wake up in the morning, take time to become conscious of any dreams lingering in your mind. Write them down straight away, and in as much detail as you can recall. Remembering that dream-language is symbolic and most often concerns aspects of the dreamer's life, offer these dreams to God and be open to insights the Spirit might reveal. Turn these into prayer. Be mindful that recurring dreams may indicate underlying concerns or personal unfinished business.

8 Offer prayers of praise by whispering, 'Jesus, my righteousness, Jesus my joy', slowly and prayerfully. As you become settled, repeat 'Jesus, my_____', filling in the blank as things come to mind. Don't worry if the words that rise up don't make grammatical sense, or surprise you: don't organize them, just offer them.

9 As you listen to a preacher or speaker, seek to 'hear' what it is that is important to them. What are the intentions and aspirations behind the content of the words they speak?

10 Think of an issue in family or church life that engenders very different responses from various individuals. Take time to imagine yourself occupying the various points of view, feelings, thoughts and ideas represented. Afterwards, allow some moments for these perspectives to be held within you. Does any potential for unity emerge, perhaps at a level the different individuals involved are not seeing?

11 In the evening, prayerfully *review* your day. Allow the Spirit to bring to mind events, feelings, thoughts and memories, and be open to seeing meanings and undercurrents you may have missed at the time. Ask God to bring to light what is most significant and offer prayers around whatever emerges.

12 In the morning, prayerfully *preview* the day. Bring to mind your anticipated plans, activities and expectations, and the people you might meet as the day unfolds. Be open to insights, from divine hunches to words of Scripture – however unexpected in the light of what you think may lie ahead.

13 Call to mind three favourite stories from whatever source – Bible, fiction, your own family history or friends' anecdotes. Muse on them, reflecting on what they have in common. Are there underlying themes and meanings? Reflect on how these might connect with your own life-story, with its hopes, fears, dreams and fulfilments.

14 Imagine you could choose to be endowed with one superhuman ability, e.g. to become invisible, being able to fly. What would you choose, and why? How would you use this power? What would it mean to you? And what does your choice say about you?

15 Carry a notebook round with you, and whenever an idea about something pops into your mind, jot it down, however irrelevant or off the wall it seems. Find some time later to review what you have written, and see if there is anything that could be fruitfully used.

16 Watch or look at advertisements, with an eye to the images associated with the different products. What underlying messages are the advertisers seeking to convey? What values and meanings are they trying to attach to their product? Can you think of alternative images that would more accurately reflect what is being sold?

17 Imagine what song-title or theme tune you would choose to represent your closest friends or family members. Or even yourself.

18 Describe what your week has been like in terms of colours and shapes, aware of what these signify to you. You may like to draw or paint it. Imagine the week ahead and what colours and shapes you anticipate will represent it. Draw or paint this as well. At the end of the week, look back at what you depicted and reflect on how your experience matched your expectations.

19 Think of someone who evokes something negative in you – fear, discomfort, disrespect, dislike. List the characteristics you tend to focus on that affirm your reaction. Now seek to discern characteristics you might have overlooked that would evoke a more positive response. List these. Can you shift your perspective on the person by focusing on these instead?

20 Listen to a piece of classical, instrumental music, and as you do so, allow images to spring to mind. You may wish to draw or write down phrases about them as you listen. What meaning do they have for you? How do they connect with the music and with you?

Before we look at some activities, a brief portrait of the *Judging* functions may help us identify them more clearly; see Table 8.

Extraverted Thinking (Te)

When we use Extraverted Thinking we are choosing to analyse and organize the world around us according to logical systems. We plan tasks, set measurable goals and achieve results.

1 Read Psalm 73. Consider the Psalmist's anger at the 'prosperity of the wicked' (NRSV) and their apparently good standing among the people (vv. 10, 11), as he struggles to understand this unjust state of affairs. What resolution does the Psalmist reach through the course of the Psalm? What injustice evokes your anger? Express your reaction honestly to God in words in your own 'Psalm', and continue to wrestle the issue through with him to come to a personal resolution.

2 In a group or with a partner, read Ephesians 1.3–14. Draw up a list of the ways God has dealt with and blessed his people

Table 8 Judging functions

Attitude	Extraverted	Introverted
Thinking	**Te** Seeks to analyse and organize Makes plans for action in outer world Prefers being decisive Works to clear, external, logical rules Values efficiency in execution Systematizes outer world	**Ti** Seeks to analyse and understand Creates structures in reflection in inner world Prefers remaining open-ended Attends to complex, internal logical principles Values precision in expression Categorizes inner world
Feeling	**Fe** Seeks harmony with others Shares values openly Outgoing: responsive to others' social needs Influential communicator Loyal to friends and wider groups Wants the world to realize their values	**Fi** Seeks harmony within self Keeps values private Reserved: shows warmth to select few Quiet influencer Loyal to what they personally value Wants to realize their values in the world

through Christ, organizing what you find under headings of Past, Present and Future. What consequences do these things hold for how we live out our faith today?

3 Read Luke 11.2–4, focusing on v. 2, 'Your kingdom come.' What are the key principles on which God's Kingdom operates? Where do these clash with how your work-place or local community runs? How can you play your part in proclaiming Kingdom integrity and challenging worldly systems? Identify one measurable goal in bringing your community more into line with God's justice. Assess the resources and strategies needed to achieve this, and do what you can to instigate appropriate action.

4 Join a theological or Bible study discussion group, and determine to participate in it fully: listen to the logic of others' arguments; be willing to research, rework, think through and talk out your understanding of issues to reach your own reasoned stance in areas of debate.

5 Listen carefully to a sermon to ascertain and analyse the preacher's line of argument. On what are the preacher's assertions based – biblical text? Reason? Assumption? Experience?

Others' authority? How logical, convincing and consistent are the arguments? Does the preacher tackle complexity or avoid problems? Are you left with any questions or concerns? You may wish to follow these up with the preacher courteously and honestly afterwards.

6 How does your church or Christian fellowship group affirm the equal status of those in its circle? Is its set-up fair, accessible and inclusive for those of different ages, abilities, backgrounds and length of membership? If not, how might the inconsistencies be addressed? Devise and plan some workable ways forward, and seek ways of alerting others to these problems, alongside offering your suggested solutions.

7 Get involved in the organizing of a church event, e.g. Harvest Festival, summer fair, coffee morning. Contribute by helping clarify the goal of the event, and the resources available to make it happen. Offer to put together a plan of what needs to be done, by when and by whom, in order to enable the event to run as smoothly and efficiently as possible.

8 Draw up a personal plan for your devotional life over the next week, month or even year. This could involve a Bible-reading schedule; a structured format and set time for your private devotions; a timetable of your commitments to corporate worship or church meetings. Follow the discipline you have set yourself, whether you feel like it or not.

9 Read a current national news story and consider any consequences there might be in terms of impact on your local community, e.g. changes in the law, economic issues, a crime or social issue. Test out your hypotheses by talking to people around you, reading local papers and so on. Do any of these consequences call for an active response from local Christians as a matter of justice and righteousness? Discuss and pray about what you have found out with others in your church and take action where appropriate.

10 Does the church you belong to have a Mission Statement? If so, examine its rationale to understand its links to your particular church context. To what extent would a newcomer be able to discern the Mission Statement in action? If your church does not have a Mission Statement, what would be an appropriate choice from what you observe of the principles and priorities evident in the way it is run?

11 Read Micah 6.8, and its call 'to do justice, and to love kindness, and to walk humbly with your God' (NRSV). Determine to apply these injunctions as consistently and specifically to every action you undertake throughout your day. In the evening, review your progress, evaluating what difference your conscious, deliberate adherence to those three principles meant to what you did and how you did it.

12 Consider taking on a new activity, e.g. an evening class. Assess what time this commitment would take up and analyse how you could budget for the hours you will need, either by reorganizing your current activities for greater efficiency, or by dropping an activity that is not necessary or important.

13 Master a new skill where you can monitor and measure your achievements, e.g. learning your way round a new computer software program, improving your golf handicap or taking up a musical instrument.

14 Risk being assertive and honest by speaking up in a situation where you are inclined to be silent or fuzzily tactful, e.g. complaining about being sold faulty goods, expressing an unpopular viewpoint, or flagging up a personal need or wish.

15 Play games such as chess, Scrabble or bridge, that involve strategy and logic.

16 Consider an action you might wish to take, from choosing a holiday destination to changing your job. Examine options by assessing the consequences and impact of different decisions. Try to step back from how you feel and work objectively as you list costs and benefits of each option. What is the most logical choice to make, given the anticipated outcomes?

17 Reorganize a room in your home, e.g. study or kitchen, along objective principles, so that a stranger would be able to pick up easily and work effectively with the system on which you have organized things.

18 Draw up a list of life-goals and ambitions you would like to have achieved in five years' time. Break these down into manageable steps. What do you need to do now that will take you nearer your longer-term aim?

19 Plan a supermarket shopping trip with maximum efficiency in mind, taking account of cost and time involved. This will involve listing the items you need and becoming aware of how products are organized and arranged within the supermarket itself.

20 Schedule a day-trip out and work out as many contingency plans as you can for whatever may not go according to your programme.

Introverted Thinking (Ti)

When we use Introverted Thinking we are choosing to analyse and understand the world by constructing logical inner frameworks. We focus on inner principles, categorize data and develop complex internal structures.

1 Read through the Gospel of Mark, noting the different people with whom Jesus comes into contact. Identify their different responses to him and develop a set of categories that distinguish these. In which category do you place yourself? Reflect on how people might move from one category to another, and what might prompt the change.

2 Read Romans 8.1–11 in as many different Bible translations as you can. Note the distinctions between them and analyse how these affect the nuances of the text. In the light of your discoveries, which version (or versions) do you wish to use for greatest precision in your own personal Bible study?

3 Read Luke 11.2–4, focusing on verse 4 and forgiveness. What does it mean to forgive, and what does it *not* mean? Use theological dictionaries and writings to deepen your understanding and challenge your own assumptions and beliefs. What exactly is the connection between God's forgiveness of us and our forgiveness of others? Examine your own conscience before God to determine where forgiveness might be required in your life.

4 Choose a major issue in the news and read versions of the same story in different newspapers. Compare and evaluate their accounts, noting how the anticipated readership affects the reporter's slant. What can you deduce about the essential elements of the story? What facts or aspects are missing that would give a fuller picture of the truth? What would be the focus of the story if God were reporting it? Use your research and reflections to inform your prayers around the issue.

5 Identify pairs of biblical terms that are very close in meaning, and clarify as accurately as you can the distinctions between them, e.g. grace and mercy, redemption and atonement.

6 Write your personal statement of faith, as precisely as possible, in no more than 100 words. Now edit this down to 50 words.

7 Read Proverbs 3.5 and Proverbs 3.13 in the New International Version of the Bible. Contemplate what it means to gain 'understanding' and what part this plays in a person's relationship with God. To what extent are trust and understanding incompatible? Or complementary? Is the pursuit of understanding an asset or a liability in your capacity to place trust in another? How can you maintain integrity of both head and heart in your Christian discipleship?

8 Take a Christian doctrine, e.g. the Trinity, justification by faith or resurrection, and apply a four-stage process of research and self-searching to it: *explore* the doctrine to determine its basic content and point; *encounter* the doctrine to discern where you see it in your own experience; reflect on *living* the doctrine, asking yourself how you can be conformed to it; and finally turn to *praying* the doctrine, by asking how it shapes and informs your praying.

9 Examine the words of hymns, songs and liturgies most regularly used in the church services you attend to discern their underlying theology. How consistent are these with one another and what is expressed in sermons and in led prayers? Is the overall theological model cogent and consistent, or are several different categories operating under one church roof?

10 Evaluate your pattern of personal devotions, Bible study and theological reading over the last few months. What has informed your choices of approach? Are there any dissatisfactions, avoidances or limitations in your system? Develop a different model to correct any imbalances and re-stimulate your spiritual life. Adopt it and review the changes after a set period.

11 What would be your most challenging question for God? Write it down and follow up by exploring in prayer, theological research and questioning others to seek to uncover whatever you can towards an answer, however complex or uncomfortable the process. Record your progress and reflections. What do you envisage would be God's most challenging question for you? Write that down and consider how you would answer him.

12 Do some Internet research on a topic that interests you. Explore different angles by trying different terms in your search engine and collect and analyse the results. As you amass data,

can you order and shape it into your own distinct categories and headings?

13 In a debate or discussion, deliberately adopt a different position from the one you usually hold, and enjoy finding ways of arguing for it logically.

14 Set aside half your collection of books, music, DVDs or whatever else you collect, and recategorize them. Now include the rest of your collection. Do they fit these categories or do you have to add on further specific categories or redevelop the whole system to incorporate them?

15 Review the categories of your collection and prioritize which item in each category you would choose if you could only keep one. Could your assembled 'priority' category be labelled in a different way, e.g. as items with sentimental associations, particular aesthetic appeal or inspirational impact?

16 Choose a type of puzzle – Su-Doku, cryptic crossword or genre of computer games – and do some background reading to research the processes of solving them. Apply your understanding by tackling one of the puzzles.

17 Develop a blueprint for an ideal education system. What would be its essential components and key principles?

18 With a partner, take it in turns to explain how something works to the other person, e.g. a bicycle, democracy. The other person assumes the role of someone with no concept or experience of what is being described, and asks the explainer to be more precise whenever something said is not sufficiently clear.

19 Which particular aspect of others' law-breaking engenders the strongest reaction in you? State or write down why this violation matters so much. Examine what underlies your holding such a firm position: is it logic, your personal history, beliefs, assumptions or factual information?

20 Identify the core principles you would argue are most important to uphold in daily living. Analyse your own habits and behaviour in the light of these, to ascertain how consistently you abide by these principles yourself.

Extraverted Feeling (Fe)

When we use Extraverted Feeling we are choosing to build harmonious personal and social relationships. We seek to maintain these through meeting others' needs and behaving in line with common values.

1 Read Psalm 23, noticing the ways the Lord tends his people as Shepherd. Where the Psalm reflects your own experiences of the Lord's care, allow feelings of gratitude to well up and offer him your praises. Where it prompts a longing for a deeper connection with the Shepherd, express your yearning to him.

2 Read John 15.12–17. Savour the Saviour's invitation to relate to him as friend rather than servant. What does it mean to be Jesus' friend? Talk out loud to him as you would to a friend, spontaneously sharing what's on your heart. Become aware of his loving presence and response to you as you enjoy the privilege of friendship with God himself.

3 Read Luke 11.2–4, focusing on verse 4 and forgiveness. Become aware of where you may be holding on to unforgiveness towards someone who has wronged or hurt you. Express your feelings to God about this, and be open to receive the ability to forgive. Picture Jesus on the Cross, dying for your sins. Receive the release of his compassion towards you and the one you need to forgive. As you start to feel and see things as Jesus does, ask him to show you how to express a forgiving attitude towards the person concerned and initiate reconciliation where appropriate. Be willing to seek another's loving support, prayer and wisdom if your particular issue runs deep.

4 Determine to find a way of blessing everyone you meet today, whether through an encouraging word, a kind act, a courteous approach, a warm smile or a listening ear. Make every encounter personally count.

5 Invite your Christian friends round and have a testimony evening where you encourage one another by talking about your personal experience of God at work in your lives. Listen attentively to each other and give thanks to God together. Talk and pray about how you can support each other in sharing your stories with those you know who need to experience God for themselves.

6 On your own or with others, find as many relational images of God in the Bible as you can: Shepherd, Friend, Father, Mother, Redeemer, Comforter, Counsellor, etc. What do they mean to you? Which best fits your experience? Would you add any

others to describe your relationship with God, particularly when talking to your contemporaries? Talk to God about your discoveries, in prayer alone or shared.

7 Make a pastoral visit to engage with someone who is lonely, housebound or in other need.

8 Be willing to *ask* for healing prayer from others, perhaps with the laying on of hands or anointing with oil.

9 Be willing to *offer* healing prayer for others, perhaps alongside other pray-ers and involving the ministry of laying on of hands or anointing with oil.

10 Enjoy sharing the Peace at the Eucharist as an opportunity to affirm others, taking their hand, smiling and looking them directly in the eye as you warmly wish them God's peace.

11 Take time to talk with others at church with an eye to discerning their particular gifts and encouraging them to contribute their unique ministry to church life. As well as enriching those around them, this will bring them a greater sense of belonging to the wider group.

12 Widen your circle. Each day determine to speak to someone new, or engage in a longer conversation with someone you see every day but don't usually make time to talk to, from a shop assistant to your next-door neighbour.

13 Rekindle an old friendship or revitalize an existing one. Make a phone call, write a letter, send a card or e-mail to let someone know how much you appreciate and value them. Be creative but not inventive!

14 Practise co-operation. If you are in a group, give way to others and go along with a group decision (in a matter of preference rather than an issue of conscience), for the sake of harmony.

15 Listen for the heart. Try to discern where another's feelings lie about an issue, whether communicated through words or behaviour. Give feedback to let the person know you have heard their feelings and acknowledge their importance to that person.

16 Observe the ways that people at your work-place interact with each other. What are the group norms and the appropriate ways to behave? Imagine you are giving advice to a newcomer on how to behave to fit in. What would you need to tell them?

17 Clarify the values you hold most dear, and identify the three people who have been the biggest influence on you in shaping

them. If appropriate or possible, you may wish to tell them how important they have been in your life.

18 Think of someone you know whose values seem to clash with yours. Talk with them to find out what makes them tick. Elicit their trust through empathic listening, warmth and openness to gain a deeper understanding of where they are coming from.

19 Try to find ways of helping those in your circle who are judging one another harshly towards greater acceptance of each other. Employ your most tactful and gracious means of offering a more understanding and positive insight into the person being criticized.

20 Observe one area where you could provide meaningful practical support to a family member or close friend: paying a bill, picking up some shopping, walking the dog, offering a lift, etc. Do it with warmth.

Introverted Feeling (Fi)

When we use Introverted Feeling we are choosing to preserve our inner harmony. We seek to maintain this by exercising personal integrity and living in line with our deepest personal values.

1 Read Romans 8.23–27. Call to awareness whatever prompts in you a response of thanksgiving and praise. Allow the Holy Spirit to stir joy and gratitude in your heart and let these feelings become your prayer as you release them to God. Turn to intercede for others, by focusing on troubled situations where you cannot work out how to pray. Be open to the Holy Spirit's touch deep within and experience whatever emotions emerge from places too deep for words. Pray with these feelings: offer them to God as expressions of his heart for the issues that concern you.

2 Read Luke 19.41–46. Identify with Jesus' emotions and behaviour as he looks over the city of Jerusalem, and then encounters the traders in the temple. Imagine Jesus looking over your own town. What would he see and how would he feel? Imagine him entering your church. What emotions and response would this sight evoke in him? Turn whatever feelings

and insights emerge into prayer, however passionate, for your community. Be willing to move from prayer to action by standing up for Christ-centred values where appropriate.

3 Read Luke 11.2–4, focusing on verse 4b, the 'time of trial' (NRSV). Put yourself in the position of those facing such times in whatever form they come: spiritual, mental, emotional, physical or material. Be open to the feelings experienced by people in these situations, and aware of those you know who are in tough times right now. As you sense their emotions, pray for them. When you next see or make contact with them, gently check out whether you picked up their feelings accurately, and express your empathy and support.

4 Explore and express your relationship with God through words, pictures or music: keep a spiritual journal, write a love-letter to God or a praise poem; compose a song; create a drawing, painting or collage of whatever stirs your spirit.

5 Savour the experience of silent unity wherever it occurs in corporate worship, e.g. during or after the administration of the Eucharist. You could explore this further in a small Christian group, perhaps lighting a candle and spending some moments in shared silence at the start or close of a meeting.

6 Notice someone at church whom you sense is in need of support, and sit alongside them if possible as a silent, caring presence. Seek to tune in to how they are feeling. You may wish to ask quietly how they are, offering a sympathetic listening ear if needed.

7 List some of the key decisions in your life, and examine them in the light of your values. Does a consistent picture emerge, or have you sometimes acted out of kilter with your own core values or faith? If so, reflect on any consequences connected with the decision concerned, and take on board what the experience has taught you. Where necessary, forgive yourself and receive God's forgiveness.

8 Take some time to be a 'Son-worshipper'. Simply rest in the radiance and warmth of the Son's presence. Consciously open yourself to receiving his love, joy and peace. If you sense any anxiety or dis-ease within, bring it into the Son-light, and let Jesus shine his healing mercy upon you. Enjoy being at one with him and at peace within yourself.

9 Find a soul-friend or prayer-partner. Set up a regular time to-gether to share the joys and struggles of your personal Christian journeys and support each other in listening and prayer.

10 Read a human interest story in your national or local news-paper. Put yourself in the shoes of one of the people involved to identify with how they may be feeling or experiencing their situation. Sense God's compassion for them. Allow whatever touches you in this process to guide your prayers.

11 Identify the values you feel most strongly about, and see if there is a church activity or ministry, charity or other cause with which they line up. Get involved and offer your support, to channel your passion and energy into a worthwhile and fruitful direction.

12 Identify times when you have felt particularly angry – perhaps to an extent that surprised even you – and reflect on what pro-voked your anger. What values were violated to cause such a strong reaction? How aware are you generally of the personal importance of these values to you? What difference might this insight make to your day-to-day living and decisions?

13 Enjoy reading biographies, and let others' stories engage, inspire, warm, humble, amuse and move you. Reflect on their values, relationships and experience of living in a different landscape from your own. Imagine yourself in their situation, with their feelings and outlook. As you tune in to these, how sympathetic do you become to the choices and actions they made in their lives?

14 Nurture your closest relationships by spending time with those for whom you feel most love. Foster one-to-one, heart-to-heart conversation and ways of sharing and caring. Where your circle includes cherished pets, take some time to bond with them as well.

15 Have a few friends round for a small dinner-party and exchange confidences as part of consolidating and deepening these relationships.

16 Become aware of where some of your personal values may clash, e.g. caring for another's welfare alongside respecting their free-dom to choose their own course; being totally honest alongside seeking never to hurt another's feelings. Reflect on where such conflicts surface, and how you might resolve them creatively to maintain your integrity.

17 Work at being graciously assertive where needed to keep your outer actions in harmony with your inner preferences and your sense of what is right. If you find this challenging, ask a trusted friend to help you. This could be through listening and encouragement, or by doing some role-play, where you can practise saying no to requests, or expressing your wishes with warmth and firmness.

18 Increase your emotional vocabulary: tune in to how you and those around you are feeling. Practise paying attention to different emotional states, and consider how you would describe them in a way that distinguishes between them.

19 Foster your emotional discernment by trusting your feelings as indicators of important values and as potential guides to right action. Listen also for their source: take time to test out whether an uncomfortable emotion is a sign of something within you that needs addressing, or whether you are picking up another's emotional upheaval.

20 On a piece of paper, draw a series of circles, one inside the other. Label them from the inside one outwards, indicating yourself at the centre and moving out through immediate family to faith community, town and beyond. Reflect on your personal values. Where these are shared by members of a wider circle, write them in the appropriate space; where they are personal to you alone, write them in the centre. Reflect on how your values both connect you with and distinguish you from those around you.

7

Applying type to spiritual direction

◦•◦•◦

Not just us

Much of this book has looked at applying our understanding of personality type to our individual spiritual direction. We may need to remind ourselves that whatever our route, we share a common Christian destiny: to know God and to mirror the character of his Son. We can all aspire towards reflecting Christ's character, as opposed to adopting his personality. Indeed, the latter would be impossible, as we cannot know what Jesus' personality actually is. It seems logical to suppose the incarnate Jesus had an inborn personality profile. (Which hand did he use to write in the dust when the Pharisees brought him the adulterous woman?) Yet in his perfect self, Jesus used the preference appropriate to the occasion. 'Tempted in every way, just as we are',[1] he presumably knew the demands of choosing to operate in his less-preferred aspects.

Gospel examples of Jesus using different preferences enable anyone to find evidence that Jesus is 'just like me'. What is more important, though, is how Jesus, as a whole and integrated personality, affirms each preference. He gives no excuse for the Spiritual 'Typism' that judges one as more 'spiritual' than another. As we become connected with others on our Christian journey, we increasingly face the challenge of coming alongside those different from us, and learning to appreciate and affirm their particular gifts.

As we now turn to reflect on using the MBTI® instrument's insights in supporting others in general, and interacting in spiritual direction in particular, we need to start with a couple of caveats.

Handling categories with care

I once read that a US company was requiring its employees to sport a badge displaying the four letters of their Myers-Briggs®

personality type. This illustrates a potential Myers-Briggs pitfall: getting carried away by categories. We may become so captivated by discovering our personality profile that it becomes all we see. If we wear our type on our sleeve, everything about ourselves and others is reduced to four letters. This might be described as the 'adolescent phase' – a sort of temporary psychological infatuation with the Myers-Briggs model that puts us in danger of boxing ourselves in and limiting our potential for growth.

The panoply of created humanity, fearfully and wonderfully made, can never be wholly encapsulated under 16 headings. For a start, the variety of different preference strengths among those with the same reported personality type overall is just one reason why some type-alike people seem to have more in common than others. It's well said that every **ISTJ** is the same as *every* other **ISTJ**, like *some* other **ISTJs**, and exactly like *no* other **ISTJs** (and that goes for every type).

If one Myers-Briggs pitfall is to jump aboard the categorizing bandwagon, its opposite is a wholesale rejection of any description that smacks of defining a person as a 'type'. There may be a sound spiritual rationale underlying such category allergy. For some, the MBTI Type Grid looks too similar to a horoscope chart, and the apparent association rightly raises some concerns: linking the concept of inborn personality preference to star-signs could lead towards a fatalistic approach that downplays our free will and personal responsibility.

However, MBTI types neither correlate to star-signs nor predetermine our destiny. Indeed, the MBTI model can open up a greater awareness of choices we may miss through unconsciously seeing things only through our own type lens. Though we have not chosen our inborn personality profile any more than we've selected our eye-colour, what we do with our psychological inheritance is very much up to us. We are not 'type-cast'.

Excessive caginess about categories may point to issues we need to resolve in our own selves. Do we fear being known or accountable in any way? Are we avoiding looking at who we are? If we are too reluctant to be pinned down or own our identity, we may lack the secure grounding of self-knowledge from which to move on in our journey.

A tool to use, not abuse

'Type', it has been said, 'is not an excuse for abuse.' This is a wise rejoinder to the concern of some that the MBTI model is soft on sin. However, Myers and Briggs are silent, rather than soft. Personality typing may reveal our preferred approach, but it cannot justify how we choose to behave: because God affirms who I am, it does not follow he endorses all I do.

Of course, selfish human beings have insisted on imposing their own way at others' expense long before they could blame Myers and Briggs. But one misapplication of the MBTI model is as carte blanche for stubbornly exercising our preferences regardless of others, under the banner of being true to ourselves – 'I don't think about others' feelings, I'm **T**,' or, 'You can't expect me to finish a job, I'm **P**.' If not allowing anyone to cramp *our* style means we start to crush that of others, it's time to rethink how we're applying our understanding of type. Rather than giving us an excuse for selfishness, the MBTI instrument can open up avenues of service, as we see where we can make the effort to step outside our preferences towards those who differ from us: where **I** has the courage to speak up and not frustrate **E**'s desire for communication, or **N** works at attending to practical details for the sake of a fellow **S**. We can choose to submit our personality type to the law of love.

Some find it helpful to see the Myers-Briggs Type Table (see p. 24) as a house – perhaps even drawing a roof over it, to highlight that it is more a home than a filing cabinet. At home, we are most at ease in our own room, but when relating to others we may need to decide whether it's 'my place or yours', and adapt our approach accordingly.

The Myers-Briggs Model in spiritual direction

The Myers-Briggs profiles in this book have been presented from an affirming angle, and intentionally so. Christian spiritual direction is not a problem-focused or short-term crisis intervention, but a slower-paced series of more widely spaced encounters over an extended period of time to support a fellow-believer's ongoing faith journey.

As we deepen our connection with Christ, we see ourselves more in his light, bringing an impetus to fulfil all our created potential.

Gordon Jeff urges a spiritual director to encourage this process through loving acceptance, and being 'constantly alert to abilities and talents and insights lying dormant in the directee, just waiting to be freed for use'.[2] In this sense, the MBTI model's rationale is helpful in emphasizing each type's gifts and potential.

If you are seeking a spiritual director for support on your own Christian journey, you may want to reflect on the questions below:

For a directee

1 How prominent do you want an understanding of the MBTI model to be in the spiritual direction process?
2 What qualities and/or qualifications are most important to you in a spiritual director?
3 Would you want your spiritual director to share your own personality type, or have different preferences from yours?

If you regard the MBTI instrument as potentially fruitful in your Christian journey, you may wish to attend a Myers-Briggs workshop first, and then prayerfully process the results alone or with a suitable spiritual director. Does 'suitable' for you mean an informed and sympathetic listener or a qualified practitioner? Would you prefer a director who knows *about* the shadow side, or one who has clearly worked *with* it on their own journey to Christian maturity, whether or not they describe this in Myers-Briggs terms?

When it comes to matching our type with another, whatever the partnership – spiritual, marital or professional – the more similar we are, the more easily we understand each other. If you are feeling alone in your Christian experience, you may value being heard on the same type wavelength, though type-alike partners can also share blind spots.

A type-different partnership may require more work in forging a connection, but could offer a stimulating alternative perspective and challenge to growth. How might it be to meet your shadow in your spiritual director? As an **NF**, I have – sometimes reluctantly – benefited from an **ST** director's ministry of drawing me back to factual reality from occasional meanderings into fuzzy idealism.

Offering spiritual direction

Since some see the MBTI instrument as *de rigueur* for those training in spiritual direction, how might the director use it? At the very least, it may foster awareness that different personalities approach spiritual direction with varying expectations, needs and abilities to engage. Some of these are presented in Table 9.

Table 9 Those coming for spiritual direction

Preferences	*may bring...*	*may need help in...*
E Extraversion: Talk it out	Willingness to be known, to express thoughts and feelings.	Staying focused on inner processes; slowing down to listen and reflect.
I Introversion: Think it through	Willingness to reflect at depth; appreciation of a one-to-one dialogue.	Trusting the confidentiality of the setting; putting inner thoughts into words; gaining courage to act in the outer world.
S Sensing: Specifics	Particular issues of concern; readiness to engage with God in the here and now; concern for practical application.	Gaining an awareness of overall patterns to address beyond the detail; seeing fresh approaches and setting future aims.
N iNtuition: Big picture	Focus on future possibilities; desire for change and growth; readiness to do things differently.	Ensuring they are not swept away by wide-ranging, idealistic aims; translating new vision into actual concrete areas to work on.
T Thinking: Logical implications	Determination to examine their lives under the spotlight of God's truth, however tough the process; a spirit of challenge.	Reckoning with the personal factor; accommodating human needs and being gentle with their own and others' frailties.
F Feeling: Impact on people	Longing for richer personal relationships with God and others; a spirit of co-operation.	Affirming their value for who they are, not what they do; learning to say no to unreasonable demands despite others' disappointment.
J Judging: Joy of closure	Commitment to faithful meeting attendance; a desire for a definite outcome from the process of direction.	Letting go of existing routines or duties where needed; considering all the options before deciding on a particular course of action.
P Perception: Joy of processing	Playful willingness to explore; engagement with the experience of direction; openness to whatever emerges.	Choosing one way forward and holding their course; following through their intentions; coming to meetings on time!

For a director's reflection

1 How far do you want to use the MBTI model yourself in your own journey?
2 What challenges does it present to you?
3 How important is it to talk in MBTI terms with a directee?
4 Do you want to use your understanding without introducing the MBTI model overtly? Or encourage your directee to attend a Myers-Briggs workshop?
5 How will you ensure your knowledge is at depth and accurate?

There is no one personality type that can be a spiritual director any more than it's the case that only certain personality types should do certain jobs. However, the MBTI instrument highlights what different preferences may contribute to the process, and where they may need to take particular care. See Table 10.

At whatever level you may wish to integrate the MBTI instrument into spiritual direction, the following considerations may be useful. Sensitive spiritual direction involves more than prescribing a few prayer exercises based on someone's reported personality type as the *de facto* way forward!

Deepen your own understanding

Use the MBTI instrument as part of your own personal development and be aware of your type's aptitudes and blind spots in spiritual direction. Talk with other type-minded folk to gain insight into other types' experiences. Foster an appreciation and respect for the value of all types. Read, research and reflect. (See Suggestions for Further Reading on p. 153.)

Consider how different models of prayer and Christian spirituality relate to various preferences. For example, the Ignatian Method of Meditation, emphasizing internal recall of specific sensory details in a Gospel scene, has been seen as a suitable SJ exercise (though for some Ss, even this is a bridge too far in terms of using imagination).

Table 10 Those in the role of spiritual director

Preferences	may offer . . .	may need to watch . . .
E Extraversion: Talk it out	Ability to create an immediate rapport; a focus beyond the internal to connection with the wider world.	Having patience with the reflective process; allowing the other sufficient silent thinking space; not intruding with own story.
I Introversion: Think it through	Ability to tune in to the depths, and stay with the complexities of the inner world.	Communicating challenge directly and verbally; remembering to facilitate the outworking in the world of action.
S Sensing: Specifics	Attentiveness to the facts, body language and specific detail of the directee's presentation; a grounding in practical reality.	Becoming so focused on present and past and what is, at the expense of seeing what could be and options for change and new possibilities.
N iNtuition: Big picture	Wider vision, hope and optimism for the future; a willingness to envision with new possibilities and directions.	Vague pictures and dreams in unclear and unspecific language; not providing enough support in working at specific steps to be taken.
T Thinking: Logical implications	Clarity of analysis; a willingness to work with difficult and complex issues without avoidance.	Looking to solve a problem at the expense of taking time to engage with the person, and support their movement.
F Feeling: Impact on people	Communication of compassion and concern; an ability to stay with the person's feelings.	Difficulty with allowing the person the necessity of being uncomfortable and facing tough truths; hard to say no.
J Judging: Joy of closure	Structure, boundaries, aims and goals – bringing a sense of purpose.	Holding God and the other to a timetable; resistance to re-evaluation and allowing the Spirit some spontaneous space.
P Perception: Joy of processing	Openness, freedom and permission to explore and venture into the unknown without setting an agenda.	Facilitating the other in making choices and facing accountability; preparation for time, holding boundaries and mutual commitments.

Look at your church worship through the type lens and reflect on which preferences are met where, and how. Widen your spiritual vocabulary by exploring other approaches to prayer and ways of connecting with God.

Listen for connection

Listening is fundamental to discernment in spiritual direction – to the other, to God and to oneself. Familiarity with the MBTI model can introduce another dimension, as we seek to 'hear' something of another's personality type.

Listen for how the directee connects. How does he present his relationships with others, himself, God, his environment – and with you in the room? What patterns and characteristics emerge? Do these highlight particular preferences? Where are the disconnections that could indicate a neglected shadow side?

Beware of trying to guess-assess another's MBTI type, and especially of telling them your conclusions. No qualification allows one person to tell another what they prefer! Besides, how we appear to behave may not be who we inwardly know ourselves to be, as in the case of the manager whose reported **ESTJ** profile was the exact opposite from who he finally realized he was. His working life so required him to rely on preferences opposite from his 'best-fit' type that he spent his days living out of his shadow side. As a result, he lost some connection with his true self, and initially assessed himself inaccurately. How soon would *we* have realized an **INFP** was sitting in front of us?

The closest you might helpfully come in revealing the type-information you are observing might be to feed back that you are hearing the directee expressing a particular preference. This may lead to an exploration of ways forward along this line, or suggest the possibility of its unnoticed alternative.

Listen for continuity

Listening for the continuity of the directee's journey is also important. What key influences in upbringing and life-decisions have brought her to this point? Where is she now, and where has she experienced God meeting with her most significantly on the way?

In terms of personality type, we have already noted how our natural development may be interrupted or distorted by our life-experience. For those whose inborn preferences have not been nurtured, the Christian faith-journey may be a longed-for release into who they really are. Affirming and strengthening their preferences is the next stage in laying hold of their true identity in Christ.

The opposite scenario may also form a starting point. Some people may have grown up confidently rooted in their 'best-fit type', and integrated this with a strong sense of Christ's acceptance of their whole selves – including their unseen and potentially shameful places. This may have readied them for the next stage of exploring their shadow side, without fear of failure hindering their willingness to risk vulnerability and the tears and fireworks that may result. At mid-life we may especially sense that our settledness needs stimulation to avoid stagnation. Ultimately, the consequence of avoiding the shadow is to stay in the shallows.

Listen for context

All our lives interconnect with others. Listening for context in spiritual direction might mean tuning in to aspects of life such as family, church and work circumstances.

Where is God for the directee in these arenas? What are the limitations, opportunities and frustrations of each? What needs to change outside and what inside? What impact might the directee's development have on those around? Do some constraints need to be accepted? If so, how can the directee work in and around them?

Here, the MBTI instrument might be useful in discerning where personality preferences are being met or frustrated by the directee's current life-situation. It can enable a greater patience in tolerating what is 'just not me', or suggest some alternative avenues of fulfilment.

This may mean simply validating the way of praying the directee is finding meaningful, but whose Christian context does not recognize as sufficiently 'spiritual'. For example, **NT**s who pray through theological reflection, or **SF**s who pray through practical service of others, may be relieved to feel set free from the **NF** prayer-mould of those most predisposed to write books on the subject!

We also need to take note when someone is experiencing upheaval or loss. This is not a good time to introduce the MBTI model. At such times we may seem like strangers to ourselves, and too eager an application of personality type insights might bring further disorientation. Once people have weathered the storm, they may find understanding their personality type helps them make sense of distressed behaviour that they felt was 'not like me at all', but was actually their shadow personality breaking through under stress.

The 1 Corinthians factor

Whatever level of MBTI expertise we achieve, we can never apply a failsafe formula to how God may lead his children. Our preferences may suggest our course, but 'God's foolishness is wiser than human wisdom.'[3] If Jesus obeyed his Father by setting aside his divinity for our sake, we too may be called to lay down our preferred ways of operating to obey Christ in a particular ministry, at least for a season.

It may also be that a person's healthy *spiritual* personality profile is at variance with his or her overall reported type. We need to set aside our assumptions and listen. Some people live their everyday lives according to their 'best-fit' type, but find that aspects of prayer and worship on their less-preferred side hold most meaning for them. God will not be corralled, and moves across our boundaries as easily as the risen Jesus passed through the walls of the upper room to meet the disciples.

Setting one another free

Our most important goal in spiritual direction is to set the directee free in Christ. It can be all too easy to look through our own preference's eyes, unconsciously seeking to create others in our type-image, and foisting our own spiritual template on them, rather than enabling them to live fully as themselves.

Going down an inappropriate spiritual route can prove to be a costly cul-de-sac. Too many Christians have endured unnecessary burdens of condemnation and inadequacy in struggling to make spiritual approaches that have blessed others work for them. Gordon Jeff comments on those who have felt oppressed by directors who 'tried to push (them) onto their own particular path, instead of helping them grow into the unique individuals they have it in themselves, under God, to become'.[4]

Sensitive and receptive spiritual directing is alongside the other and does not play God. We need to be empathic and willing to set aside our own preferences to enter another's world. This may involve drawing on our own less-preferred aspects to giving others what they need, not just what we're comfortable with offering.

Coming to church

While spiritual direction brings us alongside personality differences one-to-one, church life connects to the wider Christian community. Exploring church and type is a book in itself, but essentially it raises issues of seeking to be similar and dealing with difference.

Given how 'we revel in being with those who are like ourselves',[5] we are likely to have chosen a church whose practices are most closely in line with our preferences. So is it good to be in a 'best-fit' type-alike fellowship? Some would say yes, as the Church universal encompasses all who follow Christ, so it is fine that the church local reflects just part of the glorious diversity of the whole. Others would argue that since, through the Cross, Jesus has broken down the barriers between God and humankind, so there is now 'neither Jew nor Greek' but we are 'all one in Christ Jesus', we are called to express that diversity by engaging with difference.

Such an issue may be raised in spiritual direction where the directee has become unsettled in her church. It may be she is not worshipping in the church of her own choosing, or the church to which she belongs has changed – or she herself is changing, and what was once helpful feels so no longer.

In such cases the MBTI type lens may inform but not replace spiritual discernment. On the one hand, we have stressed the importance of finding the right route for our personality type to enable spiritual growth. On the other, we have noted how we can meet God powerfully through our least-preferred aspects – and membership of any church will face us with some of those! In spiritual direction, it may be helpful to identify what the directee feels is missing and what is needed. Are there other avenues to pursue to meet the particular need without having to disconnect from the community? If you are in a lively church, you may not be the only one who would appreciate a contemplative prayer group. Perhaps your call is to stay and serve the people by offering to set one up.

Where we are moving towards a decision to change church, we need to be willing to work this through with honesty, so we know we are not acting out of impatient individualism, or running away from our own shadow rather than facing a challenging opportunity to grow. Changing church must surely be a last resort rather than a first option. Though sometimes last resorts are necessary.

Together in God's image

As those made for connection, Christians are ultimately and inescapably part of the Body of Christ. If we want to connect to God, then we need to connect to each other, because each preference is part of an aspect of God in whose image we are made. As Keating observes, 'most of us only see a portion of reality, in terms of our personality preference. No-one of us is whole in the sense of God. We are his fragments.'[6]

Our Christian faith-journey towards wholeness will involve connecting with those aspects of God we naturally reflect, and encountering the 'otherness' of God in the preferences of those around us. The MBTI personality type model points to 'the balance, harmony and perfection of the Person of God',[7] glimpsed as the preferences of each one, made in his image, come together as one Body in Christ, joined, growing and building itself up in love, as 'each part does its work'.[8]

> Blessed be God whose word goes out and does not return empty.
> In him the active cry out and are heard.
>
> Blessed the God of deep and hidden things.
> In him the reflective keep silence and are understood.
>
> Blessed be God who formed the universe.
> In him the sensate are fed and satisfied.
>
> Blessed be God who is making all things new.
> In him the visionaries hope and are not disappointed.
>
> Blessed be God who faithfully brings forth justice.
> In him righteous minds are guided into all truth.
>
> Blessed be God who is gracious and compassionate.
> In him merciful hearts are comforted in their troubles.
>
> Blessed be God who does what he has planned.
> In him the disciplined find their boundaries fall in pleasant places.
>
> Blessed be God who rested on the Sabbath.
> In him the playful find their joy and delight.

References

Chapter 1

1 2 Corinthians 3.18.
2 A. Long, *Approaches to Spiritual Direction* (Cambridge, Grove Books, 1984).
3 G. Jeff, *Spiritual Direction for Every Christian* (London, SPCK, 1987).
4 K. Leech, *Soul Friend* (London, Darton, Longman and Todd, 1994).
5 M. Guenther, *Holy Listening* (London, Darton, Longman and Todd, 1992).
6 T. Merton, *Spiritual Direction and Meditation* (London, SPCK, 1984).
7 H. Koenig, M. McCullough and D. Larson, *A Handbook of Religion and Health* (Oxford, Oxford University Press, 2001).
8 A. Long, *Approaches*.
9 C. Keating, *Who We Are Is How We Pray* (New London, CT, Twenty-Third Publications, 1993).
10 I. Myers, *Gifts Differing* (Mountain View, CA, Davies-Black, 1980).
11 L. Francis, *Faith and Psychology* (London, Darton, Longman and Todd, 2005).
12 C. Keating, *Who We Are*.
13 Richard Rohr, *Everything Belongs* (New York, Crossroad, 1999).

Chapter 2

1 The home of the MBTI instrument in Great Britain is OPP® Ltd, based in Oxford. See <www.opp.co.uk>.
   The Retreat Association's annual *Retreats* publication also gives details of Myers-Briggs workshops being run at retreat centres across the country. See <www.retreats.org.uk>.

Chapter 5

1 Romans 7.15.
2 Psalm 139.12.
3 L. Thomson, *Personality Type: An Owner's Manual* (Boston, Shambhala, 1998).
4 John 21.1–8.
5 Matthew 9.16–17.
6 John 21.9–15.

7 John 9.1–7.
8 Luke 19.1–10.
9 Mark 1.35–39.
10 Mark 10.21.
11 Luke 5.29–34.
12 Matthew 22.1–14.
13 Luke 21.11–33.
14 Luke 22.39–46.
15 Luke 22.17–20.
16 Luke 8.43–48.
17 John 4.7–30, 39–42.
18 Luke 20.20–26.
19 John 8.3–11.
20 John 11.30–44.

Chapter 7

1 Hebrews 4.15.
2 G. Jeff, *Spiritual Direction for Every Christian* (London, SPCK, 1987).
3 1 Corinthians 1.25, NRSV.
4 G. Jeff, *Spiritual Direction.*
5 C. Keating, *Who We Are Is How We Pray* (New London, CT, Twenty-Third Publications, 1987).
6 C. Keating, *Who We are.*
7 B. Duncan, *Pray Your Way* (London, Darton, Longman and Todd, 1993).
8 Ephesians 4.16, 17.

Suggestions for further reading

Duncan, Bruce (1993), *Pray Your Way*, London, Darton, Longman and Todd.

Francis, Leslie (2005), *Faith and Psychology*, London, Darton, Longman and Todd.

Goldsmith, Malcolm and Wharton, Martin (1993), *Knowing Me Knowing You*, London, SPCK.

Guenther, Margaret (1992), *Holy Listening*, London, Darton, Longman and Todd.

Hirsh, Sandra and Kise, Jane (1997), *Looking at Type® and Spirituality*, Gainesville, FL, CAPT.

Jeff, Gordon (1987), *Spiritual Direction for Every Christian*, London, SPCK.

Jones, Jane and Sherman, Ruth (1997), *Intimacy and Type*, Gainesville, FL, CAPT.

Keating, Charles (1993), *Who We Are Is How We Pray*, New London, CT, Twenty-Third Publications.

Kroeger, Otto and Thuesen, Janet (1988), *Type Talk*, New York, Dell.

Long, Anne (1984), *Approaches to Spiritual Direction*, Cambridge, Grove Books.

Michael, Chester and Norrisey, Marie (1991), *Prayer and Temperament*, Richmond, VA, Open Door.

Mulholland, M. Robert (1993), *Invitation to a Journey*, Downers Grove, IL, Intervarsity Press.

Myers, Isabel Briggs (1980), *Gifts Differing*, Mountain View, CA, Davies-Black.

Myers, Isabel Briggs (1998), *Introduction to Type™*, Oxford, OPP.

Thomson, Leonore (1998), *Personality Type: An Owner's Manual*, Boston, Shambhala.